How To Implement Your
CAMPUS STRATEGIC PLAN

Courageland Publishing

168 East State Street
Doylestown PA 18901
sanaghan@aol.com

ISBN: 978-0-578-80562-7 (print)

Ordering Information:
Special discounts are available on quantity purchases by corporations, associations, and others. For details, contact sanaghan@aol.com

How To Implement Your

CAMPUS
STRATEGIC
PLAN

A "PRACTIONER'S" GUIDE

Patrick Sanaghan, Ed.D.

CONTENTS

About the Author

Dr. Patrick Sanaghan is an organizational consultant who works in the corporate sector, higher education, and the nonprofit arena. He is president of The Sanaghan Group, an organizational firm specializing in leadership development, executive coaching, strategic planning, and leadership transitions.

Dr. Sanaghan has worked with over 250 campuses and scores of organizations in the last 30 years. He has taught leadership to thousands of leaders in higher education and has helped over 100 campuses conduct collaborative and transparent strategic planning processes. He is the coauthor or author of 10 books, 50 published articles, and monographs in the fields of strategic planning, leadership, leadership transitions, and change management. Dr. Sanaghan also served as a board member of the College of Saint Benedict in St. Joseph, Minnesota, for several years.

Foreword

"Many people regard execution as detail work that is beneath the dignity of the business leader. To the contrary, it's a leader's most important job."

—Larry Bossidy and Ram Charan[1]

"Managers are trained to plan, not execute."

—Lawrence G. Hrebiniak[2]

I completed this book in the spring of 2020, right when the coronavirus pandemic was in full swing. I believe that this crisis is a game changer for higher education in many ways. We won't return to "business as usual" for almost all of our campuses because this pandemic has revealed many of the hidden flaws, fragilities, great strengths, challenges, and opportunities that most of our campus leaders now face going forward. It has also shown how resilient we are, how talented and dedicated our faculty can be, and how we can respond well to a crisis. It has been deeply impressive, ennobling, and hard work.

Our decision-making and governance processes need to be improved tremendously so that we can make smart decisions and take fast action. We will need to be agile, mobile, and responsive to the changes and adaptive challenges we face because they aren't going away.

I hope that this book will be a helpful resource to those people who have to get the right things done in the "new normal" we will be

---

1 Bossidy, L. & Charan, R. (2002). *Execution: The Discipline of Getting Things Done.* Currency.
2 Hrebiniak, L. G. (2005). *Making Strategy Work: Leading Effective Execution and Change.* Pearson.

living and not get bogged down with tradition, hierarchy, convoluted processes, endless debate, and antagonistic relationships between faculty and administers.

Our work is cut out for us, and if we don't get better at implementing the right priorities, many of our campuses will be in trouble going forward.

Transparency and authentic engagement will be vital in the future. We must find ways to involve multiple stakeholders in quickly prioritizing initiatives and plans, which will improve the chances of accomplishing what's really important.

This book will provide effective practices and protocols that have been tested on over 100 campuses across the country. They work, and I hope you find them useful with your implementation efforts.

Introduction

The success rate for the *implementation* of strategic plans is dismal,[3] ranging anywhere from 63–90 percent. In fact, Kaplan and Norton, of *The Balanced Scorecard* fame,[4] estimate that 80–90 percent of strategies fail due to poor execution. I tend to agree with their findings as it pertains to higher education.

Creating strategies and inspiring strategic plans is not hard work. We have many intelligent, dedicated people throughout our campuses that have powerful hopes and aspirations. But having beautiful pictures of the future is not enough; we must be able to produce them. That's the difficult part of strategic planning. We must become world class at actually *executing* our strategic plans. This will not be easy.[5]

In some ways, this book is my search for the holy grail of implementation. Why is the *doing* part so hard? I share dozens of practices and protocols I have successfully utilized on many campuses. These are not theoretical constructs but are practical, reality-based ideas that have worked on campuses throughout the country

Many of the suggested strategies take a real investment of time, attention, and effort, but I believe the payoff will be well worth the hard work invested.

I have been involved with implementation efforts that utilized approaches like the Balanced Scorecard or Six Sigma. Both have posi-

---

3   Zook, C. (2001). *Profit from the Core*. Harvard Business School Press.
4   Kaplan, R. S. & Norton, D. P. (1996). *The Balanced Scorecard*. Harvard Business Review Press.
5   Hrebiniak, *Making Strategy Work*.

tive attributes but take an extraordinary amount of time, money, and leadership attention to implement effectively. It can take *years* before you experience meaningful results. Most campuses don't have years to see the fruits of their labor—they need to see results now.

I wrote this book for the *practitioners* on our campuses. They are the real heroes, in my opinion. These are leaders who are diligent and disciplined, persistent, and patient. They are as rare as blue diamonds. It takes perspiration and aspiration to implement meaningful things. The ideas in this book will take lots of perspiration and hard work; there are no shortcuts when it comes to actually getting things done.

As I put this together, I wrote with a campus like this in mind: They have many smart, dedicated employees but lack resources. Most folks are doing a job and a half because they care about the mission, people, and places. It is difficult for them to carve out big blocks of time because there is so much to do and too few people to do everything. They might have a "planning office," but it is usually one overwhelmed person who also helps with institutional data collection and budgeting and also sells tickets at the basketball games! They just don't have money to pay external consultants; there is no real budget for this kind of external support. They understand how hard and important implementation really is and want to achieve meaningful results that serve the mission of their campus but are struggling with *how* to do this.

I share dozens of practices and protocols in this book, and my strong advice for the practitioner is: *Try one thing and see what happens.* If it works for you, then share it with others and try something else.

Throughout this book I share a lot of relevant research about implementation and execution, but this is a *practitioner's* manual, not an academic tome. The tone and tenor are informal and hopefully informative.

HOW THIS BOOK IS ORGANIZED

Chapter 1 outlines some embedded challenges regarding implementation that pertain directly to higher education institutions. Understanding these challenges is an important step in comprehending why implementation efforts are so difficult.

In **Chapter 2** I share 13 "Hard Lessons Learned" about strategic planning implementation. They come from my work on over 100 campuses. They are well earned from many successes, a fair amount of failures, and challenges met. I hope you find them useful.

Chapter 3 is about system and large group implementation meeting designs and is the heart of the book. It presents many of the practices and protocols that campus leaders have utilized to achieve meaningful results and implement their strategic plan.

Chapter 4 discusses Teams, and provides several team-based practices that will clarify alignment around goals; share a supervisory process that has helped hundreds of leaders in higher education support and manage their teams more effectively; evaluate their team meetings and improve them; and delegate responsibilities and assignments thoughtfully so that things actually get accomplished.

Chapter 5 is the "Tool Box," which provides a number of practical tools and protocols that campus implementers will find useful in creating clear goals, providing feedback on ideas, identifying who to involve in decision-making, and assigning responsibility for tasks and assignments.

Appendix I has three informal, but informative, surveys that look carefully at 1) Organizational Culture, 2) Implementation Capacity, and 3) Boundary Management. These three assessments provide a "snapshot" for implementers *before* they begin to try and move things forward. Understanding how your organizational culture influences your implementation efforts is vital to success.

Furthermore, understanding your current capacity to actually implement things is helpful so that you know what your strengths and weaknesses are before you start trying to lift things up. The "mud pies" (e.g., obstacles and challenges) are all over the place, and this survey will help you avoid most of them.

Lastly, there are organizational "boundaries" all over the place, and you need to understand the political, resource, power, and relationship boundaries that exist so that you can align your efforts with them and not have these, almost always, hidden boundaries scuttle your efforts.

Appendix II includes a description of a five-phase strategic planning process that has been used with over 50 campuses. It's deep attention to the process side of planning helps with implementation efforts later.

I also describe the "Push Agenda," which deals specifically with implementation in the final year or so of a strategic planning process and helps prioritize the most important parts of the plan, going forward. It reenergizes stakeholders so that the final year (the "push") is meaningful and people feel like they accomplished what matters and finished well.

The "Push Agenda" notion comes from my planning work with Fr. Dennis Holtschneider, who was the president at De Paul University for many years.

The **Annotated Bibliography** includes a fair amount of research about the implementation and execution of strategic plans and initiatives. I have captured and described in some detail 13 resources to consider. When it comes to implementation and execution, you need all the ideas you can get.

CHAPTER 1

The Five Implementation Challenges Unique to Higher Education

1. The Challenge of Organizational Culture

"Culture eats strategy for breakfast."

—Peter Drucker

The famous quote above by Peter Drucker, the great organizational thinker, is one of the truisms of institutional life. When you attempt to implement something, you will meet your campus' culture head on. Your culture will either hinder or help your implementation efforts. Sometimes it does both. Edgar S. Shein communicates that organizational culture is the most difficult attribute to change and that matches my experience.[6]

I used the simple description of culture as "the way things are done around here,"[7] which includes institutional values, norms, beliefs, history and how decisions get made, how conflict is managed, power utilized, and campus traditions.

The powerful role that culture plays with change and implementation efforts has been highlighted by many organization-

---

6   Schein, E. H. (2010). *Organizational Culture and Leadership.* Jossey-Bass.
7   Deal, T. & Kennedy, A. A. Kennedy. (2000). *Corporate Cultures.* Basic Books.

al thinkers.[8] They surveyed 2,200 leaders and managers from around the world and found:

The importance of organizational culture cannot be over emphasized. It can kill your implementation efforts or support them. Campus implementers need to understand the complexities of their campus culture *before* they attempt to implement their strategic plan.

In Appendix I, I provide an informal organizational culture survey that has proved helpful to campus leaders as they try to understand the positives and negatives about their institutional culture. Sharing this information widely is essential so that campus stakeholders know what the strengths and weaknesses of their organizational culture is currently. This way they can strategize on how to build on their strengths and neutralize their weaknesses.

In higher education, our many different campuses have cultures where smart, honorable, dedicated individuals work hard every day in service of the mission and values of their institution. These stakeholders prize rigor, discipline, and open debate about important issues. They care deeply about their "place" and go the extra mile to serve the students under their watch.

Unfortunately, there is a "shadow" side to many campus cultures where: There is limited tolerance for failure; a reluctance to speak truth to power, especially to the president; little risk-taking; a negative attitude toward creative approaches and doing things differently; and often an antagonistic relationship between faculty and administrators. Most campuses I have worked with simply don't like change very much.

I am not talking about change for change sake—that's a waste of time; I am talking about things like curriculum redesign, post tenure review, program prioritization and reallocation, and strategic planning implementation. These efforts take a lot of think-

---

8   Farson, R. & Keyes, R. (2002). The Failure Tolerant Leader. *Harvard Business Review.* https://hbr.org/2002/08/the-failure-tolerant-leader.

ing, time, and great effort. Unfortunately, resistance is a constant companion on most campuses, even when the need is quite clear.

I have witnessed many campuses where cross-boundary collaborative efforts (e.g., sharing best practices, identifying implementation challenges, solving problems together) simply don't happen very often. I have also experienced a handful of curmudgeons—people who are cynical, negative, and often downright mean. They can stop a process or conversation dead in its tracts, *and they know it.* One of the great mysteries of my long career is how much power we give these cranky individuals.

It will be very interesting to see how the COVID-19 pandemic and the rapid, wholesale move online will impact and influence how things get done in higher education going forward. I wonder what the self-appointed role of the curmudgeons will be in the future. Will we need them? Probably not, and I believe this will help with implementation efforts in the future.

2. **The Challenge of "Hidden Initiatives"**

Several years ago, I received a call from the board chair of a large institution. He had an interesting dilemma. Three senior leaders on the president's cabinet had left the institution over the past year. These were all dedicated, intelligent, and hard-working individuals.

In exit interviews, they reported that they felt overwhelmed with their workload and responsibilities, confused about where the institution was going, and were unable to prioritize their work and move things forward. The board chair was concerned that if this trend continued, the very best people would leave and the institution would suffer.

I was asked to conduct a series of confidential interviews with administrators and faculty leaders to identify what was going wrong. After several days of interviews, the problem became clear: Almost everyone reported that they were exhausted and concerned about making meaningful progress toward institutional goals. I also found out there were many "presidential initiatives" that were sucking up resources, attention, and time. Surprisingly, many of these initiatives were "hidden" simply because people were unaware of them. Although they might have heard about them, they were not cognizant about the scope, complexity, or resource needs of these multiple initiatives. Many people reported being in a "bind"—torn between serving the institutional strategic plan and helping implement all the different initiatives.

I then met with the board chair and president to share my findings. It was a long and difficult meeting because the president was reluctant to discuss the many initiatives that were underway. Many of the initiatives were successful, many were not, and all took enormous resources.

After a series of sensitive conversations, the president and board chair agreed to identify all current initiatives outside the strategic plan. It took several hours to list them and describe their purposes and status. We ended with a list of 31 initiatives.

There was no way to successfully implement the stated strategic plan and these resource hungry initiatives. Over a period of several weeks, we created a process that prioritized the 31 separate initiatives into one of three categories:

a. **Strategically important initiatives:** These were deemed to be successful initiatives that helped further the mission of the institution, were aligned at some level with the current strategic plan, and were clearly acknowledged by multiple stakeholders to be of great value (e.g., an effective relationship with the local school district with teacher preparation and certification; a high profile energy sustainability initiative that served the community and actually saved money). This list comprised 17 of the 31 initiatives.

b. **Nice-to-have initiatives:** These initiatives were not high profile and lacked high value but had some historical connection to the campus, made stakeholders feel proud about their participation, and could be enhanced over time. Many of these were loosely formed partnerships with the nonprofit sector and some local businesses. For example, there was a long established after school program for at-risk students that was staffed by some campus employees, but it was poorly managed by the nonprofit executive director and was not well supported by the business sector. The campus had to pump resources and people into it on a regular basis because it was a "feel good" and visible project in the community. But the partners weren't really invested in its success, gave little money to it unless badgered, and didn't seem to take responsibility for the success of the program but took credit for the campus' work and investment. For example, they would show up for the annual community dinner because it was well-publicized—essentially a photo op that the campus was paying big bucks for.

We proactively held discussions with these partners and discussed the real need for them to step up to the plate and provide more leadership and resources to these initiatives. We were successful with six out of the eight "nice-to-have" initiatives being more fully owned by the external partners. Two of them did not continue due to a lack of support.

c. **Non-value added initiatives: T**here were six of these, two of them were historical in nature (former presidents created them) and four were unproductive and dysfunctional, and still took up a great deal of time and effort.

We eliminated them over a course of a year and made sure the staff and leadership that supported them (about 20 people) were allocated to efforts directly aligned with the strategic plan.

In the end, the two nice-to-have and the six initiatives that didn't add value were eliminated. This saved money, people, and other resources that could be directed toward implementation efforts. Within a year, people saw real movement with the strategic plan. In addition, the president declared a moratorium on special initiatives for the next two years.

Most campuses I have worked with have some special initiatives—many are well-intentioned and help contribute mightily to the vision and mission of the institution. But some do not. Even schools within the institution (e.g., business, education) and departments have some of these resource hungry efforts that can be hidden from others, and many of them are considered sacred.

These are often revealed when *integration* begins to occur. For the first time, many stakeholders become aware of the plans, projects, and efforts of others throughout the institution. They realize both the opportunities and redundancies that are present. Campus leaders need to review their departmental, divisional, and institutional initiatives annually and measure their impact and effectiveness and prioritize them. Strive mightily to preserve only the best that are aligned with the strategic plan.

In Chapter 3, I will share several meeting designs that will enable you to see the "whole" system and ensure alignment and integration.

3. The Challenge of Institutional Dog and Pony Shows

On almost every campus I have worked on over the past 30 years, I have seen operational mechanisms and structures that are designed to facilitate implementation. For example, many campuses have an Institutional Planning Committee, a Budget Review Committee, an Institutional Effectiveness Committee, or a Master Plan Task Force. On paper, these look like effective processes and systems, but in reality they often fail to realize their promise. Often, these are "coordinating" groups that might share information (carefully) with each other but never get into the real and difficult strategic issues.

Even when a cross-boundary group is created (leaders from all the committees across campus) to share progress, it becomes a glorified dog and pony show. Each leader is given 10 minutes to review the progress of their respective committees and task forces. A few soft questions might be asked but it is mostly a communication vehicle and not a collaborative learning mechanism that will help drive implementation efforts.

It is what happens *during* these meetings that makes a difference. Unless they are organized—or as I call it, "designed"—carefully to share challenges, identify best practices, recognize dependencies, or seek out opportunities for leverage, they will have minimal influence on implementation. You need to craft a set of powerful questions that each person has to report out on, rather than let people share what they think is important and what usually makes them look good.

An article in the *MIT Sloan Management Review* titled, "The Pitfalls of Project Status Reporting,"[9] surfaces several "inconvenient truths" about these kinds of report outs and is well worth the read.

Unless real issues are surfaced and discussed, it becomes a missed opportunity. This can only happen if a culture of candor[10] exists on the campus. I believe that senior leadership is "the" group responsible for creating an open and collaborative culture on a campus.

MINI CASE STUDY

A couple of years ago, I worked with the president of a large land grant institution in the South. The strategic planning process created four big goals with 12 key initiatives that supported the goals. Each strategic initiative had a named owner (an implementation best practice).

The president convened all the owners once a month for a half-day meeting to review progress and solve problems together. The presi-

---

9   Kiel, M., Smith, H. J., Iacovou, C. L. & Thompson, R. L. (2014). The Pitfalls of Project Status Reporting. *MIT Sloan Management* Review. https://sloanreview.mit.edu/article/the-pitfalls-of-project-status-reporting/.

10 O'Toole, J. & Bennis, W. (2009). A Culture of Candor. *Harvard Business Review*. https://hbr.org/2009/06/a-culture-of-candor.

dent had two ground rules for the meeting and shared the following context:

"We have our work cut out for us, but I am excited to be working with such a stellar group. I will do everything I can to support the important work that you do for the university going forward.

"I have two requests: 1) When we convene I want to create the opportunity to share the success that you have experienced with your implementation efforts. 2) I also expect each leader to share their implementation challenges—the things that they are struggling with.

"I do not want dog and pony shows, where everything is wonderful. With implementation there will be problems, challenges, and missteps and I want to know about them.

If we can share the challenges, I have great faith we can solve them."

I witnessed several of these meetings over the course of a year and was impressed by participants' honesty and also how they strategized together on how to deal with the identified challenges. I can count on one hand, maybe two, the number of times I experienced such honesty about real, tough implementation problems.

We did a "Deep Dive" three years into the planning process and found that this campus had accomplished over 80 percent of their stated goals and objectives. I believe that the culture that was created in the monthly meetings was "the" factor in the successful implementation of their plan.

Elsewhere in this book, I will provide several ways to utilize these institutional structures so that participants share strategic information with each other and, most importantly, collaboratively solve problems together.

4. **The Challenge of "Nice" People Who Don't Do Much** (a counterintuitive notion)

Most of the people I have worked with on campuses are hardworking, dedicated, and intelligent individuals. But about 10 percent of the people I have encountered are "nice" people who are terrible at achieving meaningful results. We cannot afford 10 percent of our colleagues not pulling their weight.

In higher education, there is a wonderful collegiality found nowhere else. It is one of the great attractions and assets of our institutions. It also has some drawbacks. We tend to avoid "difficult" conversations about people's lack of performance and competence. I have found this is especially true when these low performers are really *nice* people.

Here's an example: I know of one Chief Business Officer (CBO) who is a poor leader and tries to run an office that is discouraged and disgruntled. But he wears the school colors proudly every day, attends all athletic events, loudly sings the alma mater with gentle tears in his eyes, his car is emblazoned with school decals, and he is a very courteous and solicitous person. You get the picture.

Unfortunately, he has been around for 20 years and still has at least a decade to go. The institution will continue to suffer from his poor leadership for a long time, unless something dramatic happens.

At this senior level of play, only the president can have the "difficult" performance conversation with the CBO. It will be a challenging situation at best but it must be done. Utilizing the advice, experience, and wisdom of your human resources department or trusted external consultants will be essential with this discussion.

Avoiding these kinds of difficult situations negatively impacts organizational culture and implementation efforts. Almost everyone knows who the poor performers are and they resent them. People know if the CBO is a champion for a strategic goal, it won't be implemented. Being assigned to a task force or work group that the CBO leads will be a punishment for people because they know their time and effort will be wasted.

One book I have found helpful in providing advice and strategies with these difficult conversations is *Crucial Conversations*[11]—it is excellent. Every leader throughout the campus should read it because with implementation efforts, difficult and sensitive conversations will emerge continually. Don't be fooled by the simplicity of this challenge; it is one of the most pervasive in higher education and needs to be dealt with directly if we are going to improve our implementation efforts.

5. The Challenge of Powerful Personalities

About 10 years ago, I was part of an important discussion regarding a failing technology implementation on a large campus. The champion of the project was a Senior Vice President (SVP) who was smart, intense, charismatic, and more than a little arrogant.

Although the vendor promised the implementation to be on time and on budget, neither were being accomplished. In fact, the project costs were approaching double the projected budget and there was no end in sight. Unfortunately, the SVP saw this project as his baby, and come hell or high water, he was going to finish the job.

The courageous president convened about a dozen leaders from across the campus to help him decide what to do. He first met with the SVP and told him he was not going to invite him to this important meeting. He communicated that he strongly believed the SVP's strong personality, mental toughness, and credibility could easily sway the group, or at least damper the discovery and debate.

The SVP was not happy with the president's decision, protested loudly, but the president stuck to his decision. He fully realized the convened group might not be as open as he needed them to be because of the SVP's presence. He took the risk of uninviting the SVP.

---

11 Patterson, K., Grenny, J., McMillan, R. & Switzler, A. (2002). *Crucial Conversations.* McGraw-Hill.

During the meeting, the president encouraged an open and honest dialogue and listened carefully to the group's input and advice. They discussed embedded costs (e.g., people, time, money) and the bind they felt with having invested so much already. It was difficult to pull the plug on such a resource intensive project.

They also discussed their concern about how the SVP would react if they decided not to continue the project.

At the end of a two-hour discussion, the president took an anonymous straw vote, and the results were 11–1 to pull the trigger. The president thanked everyone for his or her participation and advice. He then met with the SVP right after the vote to share the results of the group's discussion.

The SVP was upset and felt his colleagues were bushwhacking him. The president told him he was going to sleep on it and meet with the SVP the following morning to share his final decision. He stopped the project from going forward temporarily and told the SVP that he wanted to replace him with two cochairs going forward. The SVP was not pleased with the decision and loudly left the campus several weeks later.

This brave and thoughtful president saw the project get completed on time and under budget. His people were motivated to implement the project because now they felt it was theirs and the right leaders were in place to pay attention, listen to feedback, and treat them respectfully.

Implementation Note:

When a leader is put in charge of an important initiative, task force, or work group, their reputation precedes them. If their reputation is good, it ups the chances of success. When it is less than stellar, your results will be very poor. This sounds simple, but I have seen many people make a lightening quick judgment about the potential success of a special project, action plan, initiative, task force, etc., when they hear who has been appointed to lead things. So choose very wisely.

I almost always like to have at least two cochairs for an important implementation project. This helps neutralize the negative impact of one poor choice and gives people some hope that the work will get done.

This is a dramatic example but it happens more often than people would think. Some might think a senior team should be able to deal with strong personalities. This is true in theory but I have witnessed many senior leaders, *especially presidents*, take over a conversation, bully their way forward, and get their way, regardless of the facts. This has been my experience working on 250 campuses over the past 30 years.

Due to the collegial nature of higher education, many leaders tend not to push back strongly when they disagree with a colleague.

Understanding this dynamic, I have worked with several presidents who removed themselves periodically from a contentious discussion about campus priorities. Strategically, they let their colleagues debate and discuss issues without them, while retaining final authority about decisions. (This is what President Kennedy did with the Cuban missile crisis in the 1960s.)

In Chapter 3, I will share a protocol called "Opportunity Mapping," which is helpful in neutralizing power in a decision-making process. Briefly, it shows how to create the best criteria for making an important decision and solicits the anonymous opinions of those who are involved in making the decision. It is a powerful and productive practice for leaders who want to make the very best decisions.

The reason I highlight the "powerful personality" challenge when discussing implementation is this: There aren't enough resources to implement all the great ideas available on a campus. We need to be disciplined and rigorous about what we choose to implement because implementation is resource hungry. Understanding the influence of a powerful personality or president is an important dynamic with implementation efforts. We need disciplined, transparent protocols and practices that invite authentic participation of stakeholders as they make decisions and neutralize the influence of power and personality.

CHAPTER 2

13 Lessons Learned (a Baker's Dozen) About Strategic Planning Implementation

The following lessons come from helping many campuses implement their strategic plans.[12] Many of these are best practices, in my view, and are mostly commonsensical. But it's important to be simple and clear when it comes to implementing your strategic plan. I can't stress this enough because really smart people can make things complicated and you don't want complicated when you're doing important work. Complexity is expensive, confusing, and in my experience, rarely adds any real value.

The following notions are hard-won lessons in many ways and they come from making a whole lot of mistakes. Please pay attention to these because they can help you avoid a lot of pain and aggravation. I have used this document many times with implementation teams and we have discussed their implications for the work they will or are doing. They have found the advice very useful.

1. **Always Have a Designated Responsible Party**

   One person (a leader) must be designated as the visible, responsible party for each strategic goal. The senior team is not

---

12   Adapted from Sanaghan, P. & Mrig, A. (n.d.). Strategic Planning Implementation and Execution Survey (SPIES). Academic Impressions. https://www. academicimpressions.com/product/strategic-planning-implementationand-execution-survey/.

a responsible party, nor would the finance office be a responsible party. One person (e.g., Provost, Chief Business Officer) is a responsible party. Strive mightily to identify one person and communicate this widely across campus on a regular basis. This is also true for divisional and departmental goals and objectives. Names attached to specific actions communicate an implementation mentality.

2. Rethink Accountability

"Accountability" is a word that is thrown around carelessly on many campuses. We bandy the word about because it sounds like the leadership thing to do, when in truth, it isn't. The term can strike fear in the heart of brave and hardworking people, especially in low trust environments. When most people hear the term "accountability," they interpret it as assigning blame. Who wants that?

Instead, consider the following:

A person or team who is responsible for a *specific* task needs to have sufficient resources (money, time, information, staff, space, technology) to be successful. This needs to be discussed openly and negotiated carefully before the assignment is undertaken. No one wants to be held "accountable" when they know they don't have what they need to get the job done. Most people in higher education have learned how to do more-with-less, but sufficient resources are essential to success.

People who are engaged in real implementation efforts need *organizational support*. This is very different than resources. This could be political support, supervisory time and attention, access to senior leadership, an effective champion or sponsor for their strategic task, and the permission to engage in cross-boundary sharing and collaboration with others across the campus. When implementers know they have this kind of support, they will work hard to achieve meaningful results and be very comfortable being held accountable.

3. **Tolerance for Failure Is Essential**

    A tolerance for failure is necessary because, when it comes to implementation, mistakes will be made—guaranteed. Implementation is a *doing* and *learning* process, and mistakes are part of that experience. If people are encouraged to learn from their mistakes and are willing to share what they learn with others, implementation efforts will be vastly improved.

    This can only happen under two important conditions: 1) The campus culture has to be supportive and have a fair amount of trust present, and 2) Stakeholders have to actually get together to discuss what's working and what's not.

    This is where senior leadership has an important role. They can convene *cross-boundary* stakeholders on a periodic basis to share implementation successes *and* failures. Convening cross-boundary stakeholders creates the opportunity for real learning to take place; it is also a courageous act. Cross-boundary engagement is rare in higher education, and I think it takes real courage to actually engage people from different silos on campus. Most senior leaders are afraid of large groups where things can go wrong.

    Initially, these meetings might be difficult, even ugly, because people see how their usual isolation in silos prevents collaboration and reveals redundancy and overlap, which translates into lost opportunities. But these meetings also provide a space for people to see the possible synergies, ways to share across silos, and *learn together*. When that happens, implementation improves dramatically. This takes a tolerance for some initial messiness but it is worth the effort.

4. **Clarify the Decision Rules**

    Your staff needs to know what their scope of authority is, what decisions they are empowered to make, and when they need to seek permission. When there is fuzziness about what people can and cannot do, implementation moves at a glacial pace.

Furthermore, give people as much authority as possible. Obviously, this depends on their skill level, expertise, past track record for accomplishments, and their motivation. For decades, the notion of pushing decision-making down to the lowest levels possible has been more of a platitude than a reality.

I suggest that campus leaders read the Dennis Bakke book, *The Decision Maker: Unlock the Potential of Everyone in Your Organization, One Decision at a Time.*[13] It shows how a leader can push decision-making down to where it belongs and actually accomplish things.

In Chapter 4, you'll find a tool to help you clarify decision rules for your team.

5. **Silence Cripples Implementation**

Fear is the great crippler of implementation efforts. When there is fear in the organization, the negative impact is almost impossible to overcome. People start to hoard information, decisions are delayed, and no one takes initiative if they can help it. Do whatever you can to eliminate fear on campus.

People usually know when something isn't working, but too often they hold back and don't share that information with leaders, waiting until others speak up. Reward the courageous when they share unpleasant news about implementation.

CASE STUDY:
Student First Project

Two years ago, I was brought onto a campus to assess the undertaking of a student first one-stop-shop project that wasn't going very well. A decade ago, this idea would have been an innovation but today it is a common practice on many campuses. Unfortunately, this campus had two previous unsuccessful attempts and most believed the third attempt would also fail.

---

13 Bakke, D. (2013). *The Decision Maker: Unlock the Potential of Everyone in Your Organization, One Decision at a Time.* Pear Press.

After conducting a series of confidential interviews with staff, I discovered many staff members felt the senior sponsor of the project and the senior team didn't respect them. They were not open to feedback, did not listen to people in project meetings, delivering bad news was frowned upon, information was hoarded, and the decision rules were vague.

In short, it was a mess.

I had to deliver this tough message to the president. It was not a comfortable conversation but it was an important one. The good news is that the president created two new and credible cochairs for the initiative going forward and picked his EVP to essentially run the process. He also strongly communicated to his senior staff that he would anonymously assess the project monthly and if didn't see progress, they would be held accountable.

The lesson learned, however, was that leaders must be committed to creating an organizational culture that supports openness, honesty, and asking the difficult questions. Relying on outside consultants to find out what's not working is diagnostic of both campus culture and a lack of an ability to implement things. If there isn't a culture of candor and openness, chances of implementing strategic priorities are slim.

6. **Middle Management Is the Key to Implementation**

   This is a pervasive finding in the research on effective change-management and implementation efforts.[14] It also resonates deeply with my experience on campuses. Obviously, senior leadership needs to be committed to the strategic plan implementation, but unless the vital middle tier of managers, directors, and assistant vice presidents, and *department chairs* believe in the plan and are committed to achieving it, execution and implementation will be minimal.

   This has several implications for senior leaders:

---

14 Cross, R. & Prusak, L. (2002). The People Who Make Organizations Go—or Stop. Harvard Business Review. https://hbr.org/2002/06/the-people-who-makeorganizations-go-or-stop.

- Middle managers and leaders must be authentically involved in helping to create the strategic plan. If they can see their fingerprints on the plan, they will be motivated to carry it forward.

- Senior leaders need to convene middle managers on a periodic basis to evaluate the success of implementation efforts. I have already talked about the need for cross boundary, collaborative meetings. It is essential that the middle managers get a chance to meet, talk, and think together about their implementation efforts, problem solve, and leverage their knowledge. It will also help build the relational capital needed for implementation.

- Identify the "adhocracy" on campus. Henry Mintzberg, the great organizational thinker and theorist, introduced this term to leaders over a quarter century ago.[15]

What is the adhocracy? Every campus has an official organizational chart that identifies the leadership officers, roles, and functions (e.g., vice presidents, provosts). It helps campus stakeholders understand who does what. Then there is the *other* chart, which includes those individuals who are the *doers*. Often, they don't appear on the official organizational chart but everyone knows who they are. These doers, or adhocracy, don't seek the limelight but work tirelessly toward to goals of the institution. They are invaluable.

These highly credible leaders, often middle managers, have huge peer influence because:

- They have reputations for hard work and for getting results.

- They are deeply trusted by others.

- They follow through on their commitments and keep their word.

- They show appreciation for others and share credit whenever they can.

---

15 Mintzberg, H. (1989). *Mintzberg on Management.* Free Press.

- They care about the institution and try to live the expressed values of the institution.

- They are sought out by others when people experience challenges and problems and don't know what to do.

Senior leaders need to identify these people and engage them in thinking about implementation efforts, not just the doing part, but *how* the implementation process should be organized, providing honest feedback about implementation efforts and results and helping to problem solve implementation challenges. They tend to be close to the action and have real experiences (not theories) about what works and what doesn't. They are a strategic asset for a campus.

Fortunately, finding these indispensable leaders is not difficult. Just ask your secretaries and administrative assistants. They will know exactly who those people are because of their campus reputations and the fact that they often refer people to them for help.

Directors and Department Chairs usually know who these "go-to" people are because they rely on them for advice and getting things done in their area of responsibility.

Any time I conduct a strategic planning process, I work with senior leaders to identify these special contributors. I always want several of them on the planning task force because they are comfortable telling it like it is. They also have large peer networks and influence, and they can act as authentic ambassadors for the planning process. Periodically, these folks should be convened by senior leadership for an open and constructive discussion about implementation progress.

Implementation Note:

In Chapter 3, you will find a meeting design that shows you how to identify the adhocracy groups on your campus.

---

7. **Keep the Focus on Results, Not Activity**

Look out for the "buckets of sweat" syndrome. This is where people are running around a lot, rushing everywhere, coming late to meetings, and looking overwhelmed. You get the sense that a quiet frenzy permeates the workplace. Whenever I encounter such a situation, I become wary because the focus seems to be on *activity* and not *results*.

If you find that your department, division, or school has this crippling and ineffective syndrome, I strongly suggest you read the *Harvard Business Review* article, "Beware the Busy Manager." Its authors, Heike Bruch and Sumantra Ghoshal, conducted extensive research about organizational effectiveness and how people actually spend their time at work.[16]

Their primary finding was that only 10 percent of the managers they studied work purposefully to complete important tasks. The other 90 percent self-sabotage by busily engaging in non-purposeful activities like procrastination, detaching from their work, and needlessly spinning their wheels.

Implementation is not busy work. It is focusing on what really matters, applying great effort, applying the idea of "learning from doing," and achieving meaningful results. Recently, I facilitated a senior team conversation about the implications of this article. It took two hours, and the team members realized that they were caught in a "busyness" cycle and made a commitment to help each other out with prioritizing their work and keeping each other informed about their top priorities.

They used the framework of the strategic plan to help them do this and committed to review the plan's progress monthly.

8. **Understand the Environment We Live In**

On almost every campus I have worked, I find many people are simply overwhelmed. There never seems to be enough time to get the most important things completed. Staff struggle to get

---

16 Bruch, H. & Ghoshal, S. (2002). Beware the Busy Manager. *Harvard Business Review*. https://hbr.org/2002/02/beware-the-busy-manager.

their strategic plan implemented and are frustrated by the lack of progress.

There are two excellent books I have encountered about execution and implementation challenges and why it is so difficult to actually accomplish something meaningful. The authors of *The 4 Disciplines of Execution*[17] use the metaphor of "the whirlwind" to describe the massive amount of energy and resources necessary to just keep an organization going on a day-to-day basis.

They believe only about 20 percent of our available time and attention isn't eaten up by the whirlwind. This is an important point and rings true to me. I think the whirlwind notion normalizes the overwhelmed feeling many campus stakeholders experience.

If only 20 percent of our time is available to accomplish things, then we have to be diligent and disciplined if we want to move important things forward. This 20 percent must be used strategically. We need to focus on what they call "the wildly important," which should be the prioritized goals of your strategic plan. There simply isn't enough time and attention to get it all done. Extraordinary focus will be essential to success.

Stephen Bungay uses the term "friction" to describe the normal hurdles and challenges[18] that keep us from communicating clearly, understanding what is expected of us by our supervisors (this goes back to getting your staff on the same page), and focusing on implementation.

His important contribution is highlighting the importance of one simple question many people ask of their managers and leaders: "What do you want me to do?" People need to clearly understand the expectations of their direct supervisor and, more importantly, the rationale behind the expectation. In short, the *why*. When both elements are present, according to Bungay, people are then trusted to move forward because they understand

---

17 McChesney, C., Covey, S. & Huling, J. (2012). *The 4 Disciplines of Execution*. Free Press.
18 Bungay, S. (2013). *The Art of Action*. Nicholas Brealey Publishing.

the *what* and the *why*. It might be simple but I believe it is a game changer and well worth the read.

9. **Define the Difference Between Lead and Lag Measures**

We measure a lot of things in higher education and can often get overwhelmed with too much information and data. The challenge with implementation efforts is that you need to be able to *measure what matters*. This is not easy to do.

One of the most important things to define with implementation efforts is the difference between *lag measures* and *lead measures*. Lag measures monitor tangible results or "outputs" (e.g., graduation rates, retention rates, alumni giving) and are rather easy to measure. Another generic example is the number of sales made, which is also an output that is easy to monitor. The problem with lag measures is this: You only know if you are successful *after the fact*. I think that this is an essential point. It can take months before campus folks know if they are successful or not (e.g., graduation rates). Paying attention to the lead measures is key.

With the graduation rate, for example, you might want to increase your graduation rate 20 percent over a five-year period. You won't know how successful you are for many years. In some ways, even if you are successful, you might not understand *why* you were successful. What did you do that specifically improved your graduation rates?

On the other hand, *lead measures* are predictive. They measure how a specific result (e.g., graduation rates, sales made) will be achieved. For example, some lead measures for the number of sales made (the lag measure) might be the number of sales calls made in a week or the number of face-to-face sales meetings with clients. These lead measures are easy to monitor over time and provide regular feedback if your ongoing efforts are successful.

With lead measures, you are determining which activities that, if performed often enough, will drive the end results (increase graduation rates, which are the lag measures).

- **Lag Measures** tell us what we have achieved.
- **Lead Measures** tell us if we are likely to achieve that goal.

With implementation efforts, we need to be good at identifying the lead measures because they show the way or steps to effective implementation. It also helps people to better understand *how* they can contribute to the lag measure because there are specific steps and activities involved that help people see the connections between the two measures.

CASE STUDY:
An Unusual But Effective "Lead Measure"

I recently worked on a campus with a prominent religious affiliation. The university conducted a religious service each day at noon. Part of the campus culture was the expectation that students would participate in these services. No one was forced to attend but the expectation was present and understood by all.

They wanted to improve their graduation rate (a lag measure) and one of the lead measures they used was student attendance at the daily religious service. They found that if their students attended services regularly (more than 75 percent of the time), they had a four year graduation rate of 85 percent (which is excellent), compared to a 60 percent graduation rate for non-attendees.

They made extra efforts to positively "persuade" and influence students to attend their daily service, knowing that if they could improve attendance, it upped the chances of graduation.

Again, remember to use lead measures to help achieve your strategic planning goals.

10. Small Wins Matter

Small wins do matter. I resisted this notion for a long time and always tried to tackle the meanest, toughest implementation challenges. I was successful about half the time, which is actually a good batting average when it comes to implementation.

If you can break down big institutional goals into *chewable chunks* (small, clear steps toward the successful implementation of big goals), you will create a visible road map. The accomplishment of small, meaningful tasks and objectives will do several things: It will create a positive momentum that will take on a life of its own. People like to know when they are winning and it will help build their confidence in the process.

a. You will learn about what works as you move forward and not have to wait until the end to find out what worked and what didn't. As mentioned before, it is essential to share this learning across campus and improve everyone's implementation efforts.

b. You will develop what I call "implementation muscles." As people experience success, they will get better at implementation. They will learn how to manage their own expectations, make better decisions, allocate scarce resources appropriately, and understand what works.

c. Once again, this is where lead measures come in to play. They can highlight all the steps and activities needed to create a successful outcome. These small wins can pave a clear path to success. They also allow people to keep score and see real progress.

Implementation Note:

Theresa Amabile and her colleague, Steven Kramer, academics from Harvard, have written a great deal about creativity and innovation in organizations. Their book, *The Progress Principle,*[19] is an excellent resource about the power of making small, visible progress over time.

---

11. Focus on Conversations, Not Presentations

Implementation has a lot to do with conversations, not elaborate presentations. We get way too enamored with large-group

---

19 Amabile, T. & Kramer, S. (2011). *The Progress Principle.* Harvard Business Review Press.

PowerPoint shows about the strategic plan featuring colorful charts and graphs that quickly overwhelm folks with too much information. Presenters blast through, say, 50 PowerPoint slides in a half hour as an attempt to be efficient. Unfortunately, it is usually ineffective.

After an exhausting presentation, there is often a feeble attempt to solicit feedback ("Does anyone have any questions?"), and usually there is little real response because people are numb and overwhelmed. Mostly, they're happy that the PowerPoint is over.

We need to have a series of smaller conversations across the campus, ones where people can ask honest questions and not feel that they are at risk if they have a tough question or raise a concern about the feasibility of the strategic plan. Unless these conversations happen, leaders will not get the authentic "buy-in" they so desperately need.

Obviously, these conversations will take some time but given that the track record for implementation efforts is pretty poor, investing the time in these conversations in your departments, divisions, and units is a good use of time. When people ask questions, they are trying to make sense of things. This is good.

In large groups, many people will not ask questions or provide feedback and, often, the more verbal, extroverted participants can take over the conversation quickly. That is why smaller groups are more effective *and* efficient. You will get more participation from more people using small groups. *Never forget this.*

The key theme that leaders need to understand is this: If people can't see the implications of the proposed strategic plan in their daily work, you will find alignment elusive. People need to make the connection between the goals and what they do every day. Just by simply asking the question, "How do you see yourself contributing to this strategic goal?" and listening carefully to the answers, you will be able to determine if they get it or not.

Obviously, people need to feel comfortable answering this question, especially if their beginning answers aren't polished or perfect. It takes time and real thinking to make the connection between something the campus wants to achieve in the future and people's current daily efforts. Patience with this is helpful and, once people see the connections, they will work hard to achieve the articulated goals.

In Chapter 3, I share a collaborative meeting design that enables participants to fully engage in thinking about actually implementing the strategic plan and their specific contribution to executing the campus plan.

12. Establish a "Planning Assumptions" Document

If you are going to improve your implementation efforts, it is especially important that campus stakeholders be on the same page about two things in particular:

   a. **The vision:** *where the institution wants to go.*

   b. **A shared framework:** *why it wants to go there.*

A document called "Planning Assumptions" is one of the most effective ways to create an understandable and shared framework for the external realities facing a campus. It attempts to create an informal picture of the current and potentially future external environment.

This document is helpful in supporting "alignment" efforts because it helps campus stakeholders understand the larger context in which they live and realize that the strategic plan is effectively responding to the external events, issues, and trends. They can then see the connection between what they are currently doing with their implementation efforts and effectively responding to the external realities.

Briefly, planning assumptions are:

- Temporary estimates of your external environment over which you have no control.
- Are general, not detailed, pictures of current reality and the possible future environment.

- Not detailed facts but important information to be considered.

- Powerful and important trends that the institution needs to pay attention to.

- Issues, trends, and forces that could impact (positively or negatively) the institution.[20]

The following are some important **conceptual buckets** that can provide a framework for the planning assumptions report. These would be filled in with the appropriate information by selected stakeholders (the board, the planning task force, senior cabinet, institutional research) and can be shared with stakeholders throughout the campus.

- Legislation/regulations
- Economic trends (local, regional, national)
- Competition
- Technology
- Global and national issues
- Social trends
- Teaching and learning
- Resources and facilities
- Demographics
- Enrollment

I suggest you keep the conceptual buckets to no more than 10. This is *not* a laundry list of everything but ones that are the most important information people should have knowledge about as they implement their strategic plan.

13. **Trust Is a Strategic Asset**

Here's an important quote that I'd like you to take to heart: "Mistrust doubles the cost of doing business."[21]

---

20 Sanaghan, P. (2009). *Collaborative Strategic Planning in Higher Education*. NACUBO.
21 Covey S. R. (2008). *The Speed of Trust: The One Thing That Changes Everything*. Free Press.

Almost every president I have worked with over the past 30 years has asked me the following: "What's the one thing that will ensure our strategic plan will actually get implemented?" In fact, there is never *one* thing that ensures an effective planning process.

You need an inclusive, highly participative process where stakeholders can help craft the strategic plan, authentic faculty participation, good data, an external perspective, robust and open conversations, and much more.

But there is one factor that is essential to a successful implementation of your strategic plan: **Trust.** By itself, trust won't make your implementation happen, but without it, I guarantee you will fail. If you have a high level of trust among stakeholders, especially between administrators and faculty, you can achieve great things.[22]

When there is low trust on a campus, every detail will be debated, progress will be slow, the rumor mill will be in high gear with negative news, and people will often assume the negative intentions of others. I have been on a few of these campuses and I have found that implementation efforts will fail in a low-trust environment, even if you have plenty of resources.[23]

Senior leaders must pay special attention to the level of trust on their campus and deeply understand how to *build and nurture trust*. Building the relational capital needed to move an institution toward excellence is a painstaking and ongoing effort. It is not a one-shot deal where you solicit input and feedback every once in a while (e.g., town hall meetings, surveys) and think the job is done.

Whenever I work on a campus to facilitate a strategic planning process, I try to determine the level of trust within the institution. This is not difficult to do. You can use anonymous surveys, have informal conversations with key top- and mid-level lead-

---

22 Bossidy, Charan, & Burck. *Execution: Getting Things Done.*
23 Sanaghan, P. *Collaborative Strategic Planning.*

ers (especially the adhocracy), as well as administrative staff that know what's being said at the water cooler.

If I find the level of trust is high, I know my work will be easier and we will implement meaningful things. When I find the trust level is low, I realize how difficult our journey will be. The good news is that you can build a sense of authentic trust through an inclusive, transparent planning process.

Some of the information I share in this book speaks directly to improving trust (such as clarifying the decision rules, convening stakeholders across institutional boundaries, and being transparent). The following advice comes directly from my work and conversations with hundreds of campus leaders as they built their own campus trust and tried to successfully implement their strategic plan.

The senior leadership needs to communicate to campus stakeholders that they use the strategic plan as an agenda for action and discuss progress on a regular basis. It is important that people know their plans don't just sit on a shelf. This communication helps build faith in the plan and people come to believe that the plan really matters. It elevates the work that they do. The following advice comes from conversations with many senior campus leaders about their challenges with their implementation efforts.

Senior leaders should conduct quarterly "implementation reviews" where they highlight progress toward goals, identify problems and challenges, and ask for solutions to various issues. People usually know what needs to be fixed and how to fix it. Senior leaders need to create the opportunity for people to discuss implementation *together*. This can only happen if the institutional culture is open and honesty is valued.

Remember that learning has a price attached to it. Mistakes are inevitable and *how* people are treated when mistakes are made will make or break an implementation process. Communicate in word and deed that failure is tolerated and learning is prized. It is the concept behind the popular phrase "fail forward."

> *When you lose, don't lose the lesson.*
>
> —Dalai Lama

Implementation is a learning journey that is seldom linear with all the steps toward completion known and clear. "Intelligent" mistakes will be made, and if people are afraid to make them, you won't get much done.

Leaders throughout the campus should share the rationale behind their decisions. This might sound simple but often people have no clue *why or how* decisions get made.

- Better yet, leaders can share their thinking and actively solicit feedback from folks. Following this simple process will enable leaders to meaningfully engage stakeholders. Leadership can have rich conversations with their teams if they use the following protocol:

  1. This is my best current thinking about the decision I need to make.

  2. This is how I arrived at this thinking (e.g., what information was used, who you talked with about it, your experience and background).

  3. Now help me understand what I might be missing or what possible impacts, both negative and positive, that can you see with this decision.

Obviously, the leader has to be interested in what people have to say and be open to being influenced on important decisions:

Tell the truth, especially when there is difficult news to share. It is one of the guiding principles in leadership and hard to do. Earlier in this section, I shared a story about the student first program, when a president had the courage to convene all the people who were involved in a failing implementation effort. He shared in broad strokes what the interview data revealed. People were amazed because that wasn't the usual practice on this campus. He gained credibility and enthusiastic support at the same time.

In an "Implementation Clinic" meeting we conducted a few days later, he asked for a set of strong recommendations for moving forward and people to volunteer to take responsibility for executing them. At the end of the meeting, there was a powerful and credible action plan. It turned the project around. The road ahead was challenging, but people had faith that they could tell the truth when things were not going well and they were committed to come up with solutions *together*.

Keep your commitments and your word. It builds faith and confidence about your integrity as a leader. You cannot lead without being seen and experienced as a person of integrity. If people believe in their leader's trustworthiness, they will go way beyond the call of duty. This comes in handy when you attempt to implement the strategic plan.

Trust is one of the most enduring and fragile elements of organizational life. It is also the most powerful strategic asset you can have. Pay attention to it.[24]

FURTHER READING

For those individuals who are interested in understanding the complexity of trust, I would suggest you read the *Harvard Business Review* article, "The Enemies of Trust."[25] It explores the themes of and differences between strategic, organizational, and personal trust in helpful ways. Another excellent book that I highly recommend is *The 4 Disciplines of Execution*.[26] Here, the authors discuss the notions of "trust taxes" and "trust dividends." They also provide some strategies on how to increase organizational trust.

If you are going to attempt to implement meaningful things on your campus, become a student of trust. I believe it is the most important element in organizational life. It is also the most strategic asset you can ever have.

---

24 Covey, S. R., Merrill, A. R., & Merrill, R. R. (2003). *First Things First.* Free Press.
25 Galford, R. M. & Drapeau, A. S. (2003). The Enemies of Trust. *Harvard Business Review.* https://hbr.org/2003/02/the-enemies-of-trust.
26 Covey, S., McChesney, C. & Huling, J. *The 4 Disciplines of Execution.*

CHAPTER 3

System and Large Group Implementation Designs

I believe that the future of higher education will be saturated with complexity and ambiguity and that we will need to meaningfully involve multiple stakeholders to create effective strategies and solutions to the adaptive challenges we will face. Unfortunately, many senior leaders fall into the trap that they alone can create the answers to these challenges. Given the COVID-19 world we now live in, there will be few clear paths forward.

Senior leaders must be committed to learning how to design and facilitate large group meetings that engage people's minds and hearts as they struggle for creating effective strategies to deal with emerging and complex issues that are careening toward us.

This is especially true in low trust environments where campus stakeholders don't trust each other. These meeting designs can create full engagement and transparency and create solutions that people actually own.

The following meeting designs can be utilized with rather large groups (e.g., 20–100 people) and often take little facilitation skill. They organize people's efforts and ideas in a transparent manner (which builds trust) and produce real outcomes that are tangible to participants. Most importantly, they tap the resources, talents, and thinking of the participants.

Often, a secondary outcome, and an important one, is that they tend to build *relational capital* between participants. When people see their colleagues working hard to solve real campus implementation challenges, sharing ideas, and communicating across silos, it can build a sense of real camaraderie throughout a campus.

These designs help avoid certain people taking over a group conversation and hogging the stage; they involve and engage even quiet and introverted participants and ensure that *everyone* is heard.

IMPLEMENTATION DESIGN 1:
The "Premortem" Meeting Design

Synopsis

People often reflect on what happened after an event such as a death, organizational failure, or crisis. That's called a postmortem meeting. In contrast, a premortem meeting has people coming together before undertaking an action or initiative provides an alternative and useful perspective. First by looking forward, then backward, this design anticipates potential pitfalls, hurdles, and potholes that lie ahead that could prevent successful implementation of recommendations and action plans. This large group design is an adaptation of Gary Klein's notion of "performing a premortem."[27]

An important strategic question that should be asked for any meeting where stakeholders create action plans for implementation is "What could go wrong with this action plan?" People tend to avoid this question, especially when they have worked hard to create the action or implementation plan.

They want to create momentum by accomplishing something soon, rather than identifying the challenges to success. Anticipating what could go wrong may seem counterintuitive to success but it helps build strategic thinking and problem-solving skills as well as enhances implementation success.

---

27 Klein, G. (2007). Performing a Project Premortem. *Harvard Business Review.* https://hbr.org/2007/09/performing-a-project-premortem.

It's best to use this design a few days after a group has created an implementation or action plan. That gives the group time to digest their ideas and gain psychological distance from their implementation plans. After a few days, group members can be more objective about their ideas and more open to identifying potential challenges.

The Activity

For this activity, you need 30 participants. Create six mixed groups by asking participants to count off from one to six. This produces six groups of five participants each.

Your room should look like this:

Part One of the Meeting

1. The meeting facilitator should welcome participants and explain the purpose of the meeting: "Today we want to anticipate what could go wrong with our action plans *before* we try to implement them."

2. Communicate the following: "Imagine we are all back here one year from now. Although we have worked long and hard, *we have failed* to implement our proposed action plans as we expected. We are here today to diagnose what went wrong. We are going to look at six specific elements that blocked our successful implementation. They are:

    1. Organizational politics

    2. Organizational culture

    3. Organizational priorities

    4. Resources (technology, money, office space)

5. People

6. Communication

(This is an additional seventh element you might consider.) Here you might identify something that is outside these six elements but which is important to consider. Just have an "Other" category.

3. As you work in your groups, think ahead one year from now and anticipate some of the reasons we were *not* successful. What blocks, barriers, challenges, or hurdles can you identify that might have gotten in our way?

4. After ensuring everyone has a marker, instruct the group members to go to the theme corresponding to their number and individually print their answers to the focus question. Participants who agree with someone else's comments should indicate agreement by checking (✓) the statement. If they don't agree, they make no mark. (This design is about individual data gathering, *not* group agreement.)

   For example, for the organizational politics element, some participant statements might be:

   - "We should have prepared for our meeting with the Faculty Senate so that they became advocates for the initiative."
   - "We underestimated the deep interest that the trustees would have in this planning project and they felt left out of the process."
   - "We didn't consider the campus neighbors and how they would react to this expansion/change/project."

5. After four to five minutes, ring some chimes (or a bell or some kind of signal) and instruct each group to rotate clockwise to the next station. Participants read the new information that has already been written down and *individually* check off all the ideas with which they agree. If they don't like an idea, then they don't check it off. This way you avoid any needless debate.

It's important to communicate that each time a group goes to a new station with a new theme, they need to read the new information, check off the ideas they agree with, and then add their own ideas to the list. This way you build an evolving database.

6.   The rotations continue until each group has provided individual input for all six elements and checked off the ideas they have agreed with. This will take 25–30 minutes and will provide the group with a great deal of strategic information. The output might look like this:

Communication

1.   We relied too heavily on electronic communication that many people did not read. People on our campus prefer face-to-face interaction. ✓✓✓✓✓✓✓✓ (checkmarks indicate people's votes).

2.   We failed to keep people informed about the progress of our implementation efforts throughout the initiatives/plan/project. ✓✓✓✓

3.   We covered up our mistakes and only communicated good news. ✓✓✓✓✓

4.   We didn't solicit feedback from our campus stakeholders on a regular basis—we did it initially, then quit. ✓✓✓✓✓✓✓

5.   We never convened groups across the campus to share stories, updates, successes, and challenges. ✓✓✓✓✓

Part Two of the Meeting

7.   At this stage, there are two options. You can either assign participants to a strategic element or let them self-select an element of personal interest. Once the groups have formed, explain the task as follows: "In the next 30 minutes we would like you to come up with some strong recommendations that would effectively deal with the identified challenges for your strategic element. Please use the information we have created to inform your thinking. Use self-managed roles (refer to self-managed groups in the

Toolbox section for descriptions of the roles) to make sure your group works effectively."

8. Ring the chimes (bell/signal) after 30 minutes and ask each group to present its strong recommendations to the larger group for review and feedback. Keep each presentation to three to four minutes or it will lose energy and focus.

BREAK (10 minutes)

9. After the six presentations have concluded, each group then decides who will do what. Having a lot of good ideas isn't enough— people must commit to implementing the only the best ideas.

Prioritization Process

10. I would suggest that you use the Las Vegas voting process (please see the Toolbox section for an in-depth description of this) to identify the best ideas in each implementation element. Briefly, the Las Vegas vote is a process where each participant in the meeting is given a number of sticky dots with which to "vote" for the best ideas from a long list of suggestions. After the prioritization process has identified the very best idea for each element, then someone needs to take ownership of the priority recommendation and move it forward. This is what I call the "champion" or "sponsor" of the prioritized recommendation. This does not mean that the "champion" does all the work but they make sure the work does get done.

11. Give each group 20–30 minutes to begin to organize an action plan for their top recommendation. Now you have some beginning next steps that can start to drive action forward.

12. Reconvene the same group one week later and have each group report on the progress of their priority action plan. This communicates that some efforts are already successful, builds a sense of accountability that recommended actions will be paid attention to, and develops the strategic notion that anticipating problems before they occur is a smart move.

IMPLEMENTATION DESIGN 2:
The Systems Perspective

Synopsis

On most campuses, it is rare that people from different work groups, schools, or business units get together intentionally to plan, strategize, or collaborate. If this does happen, it usually occurs among the senior people, which doesn't help much with the actual implementation efforts.

This implementation activity enables participants to see the "whole" picture as a part of planning for the future. This activity could be part of a benchmarking meeting to determine where people are and where they are going; to look for alignment among divisions, schools, and groups; identify redundancies; and problem solve for the future.

It gives all participants a unique systems perspective or "picture" of the organization. Often, it is the first-time participants have a clear picture of what others on the campus are working on and how they can contribute to the overall effectiveness of their institution. It never fails to be engaging and enlightening.

The Activity:

On a campus, senior leadership would convene five participants from each of the following divisions:

1. Human Resources

2. Finance

3. Information Technology

4. Student Affairs

You want each group of five participants to be diverse, representing the different layers of their organization. For example: for Finance, you might want the CBO, the Controller, some frontline staff (e.g., a budget analyst or a middle manager).

Participants should be informed ahead of time that the goal of the meeting will be to share information with other work groups on the campus and to work together to leverage resources and learning. They should know that they will be able to see what other work units, departments, and divisions are doing throughout the institution and see how they can build on each other's strengths and create productive opportunities going forward.

Have a grid like the one shown below prepared ahead of time using large, 25 x 30 flip chart paper. The grid must be large enough to contain all the information generated and to be seen at a distance of 10–15 feet. It usually takes up an entire wall. In our example, with four different units participating and five categories, they would need a grid approximately 10–12 feet long and six feet high.

SAMPLE GRID

Categories/ Strategic Questions	Student Affairs	Technology Department	Human Resources Department	Financial Department
Beliefs/Values				
Four Greatest Strengths of Your Unit				
Three Top Priorities or Challenges in the Next Year				
Two Areas of Needed Improvement				
One Resource Willing to Share				

Possible Questions

Here are some sample questions that you might chose for the meeting. I would limit them to a total of six focus questions or you may experience information overload.

1. What are the three greatest strengths of your unit/group?

2. What are your unit's/group's three greatest challenges over the next one to two years?

3. What do you think are the campuses' greatest challenges over the next one to two years?

4. What are one or two best practices that you utilize, that you are willing to share with others (e.g., a practice, protocol, or process)?

5. What are your top strategic priorities for the next year or two?

6. If you could give senior management one piece of advice, what would it be?

7. What is a resource (e.g., technology, expertise, space, and offices) that you might be willing to share?

8. What's an implementation challenge you are currently facing?

9. What's an opportunity you see that would be worth pursuing?

Ask people to get into their work units (Technology, Finance, etc.). Give them 15 minutes to generate the information to complete the grid. Make sure you send the final focus questions prior to the meeting.

Next, ask individuals to go up to the grid and fill in the information for their work unit. Allow 15 minutes.

After the information has been generated, you now have an interesting picture of the wider system, possibly for the first time. Have one person from each work group do a brief presentation of the written information on the wall chart so that everyone in the room clearly understands what is on the large grid. Allow some time for clarification and questions. Below is a possible snapshot of a section on the grid.

Three Greatest Strengths of Our Unit

- Creative thinking is allowed as is taking risks.
- Our people work together well; we like each other.
- We have hardworking employees.
- We are customer centric and personable.
- Our people stay current with changing market trends.
- We are knowledgeable about our work.
- We have a good campus reputation.

After each group has presented its information, have participants get into mixed groups (one person from each department, division, and unit) and as a small team, diagnose what they have heard and seen across the four different units. Some possible focus questions might be:

- What stands out to us?
- What gets our attention?
- What are some ways we can leverage our resources?
- How can we help other divisions/units?
- What do we need to keep in mind as we plan for the future?
- Are there challenges we face that are similar?
- How do we use our collective strengths to manage the challenges?
- Are there any surprises or discoveries? Any "ahas?"
- What are the biggest challenges facing the campus?
- What Implementation challenges do we need to pay attention to?

After the groups have reviewed the Systems Grid, each "mixed" group should take 10 minutes and make two or three strong recommendations that the campus leaders should seriously consider.

It is important to remember that this group, because of its diversity and knowledge, is in a unique position to see what the organization needs to do because they are now seeing the bigger picture from diverse perspectives.

Some examples of strong recommendations are:

1. We seem to have a situation where there will be many of our people leaving pretty soon; we need to plan for this.

2. Communication seems to be an issue across our four units; we need to establish a robust and agile communication process throughout the campus.

3. Training and professional development are critical to our future. Things are changing all the time. We need to coordinate these efforts so that we don't overwhelm people. Human Resources should coordinate these activities and evaluate their effectiveness.

4. We have a lot of talented people that we need to keep here. Create a reward and recognition process for people who contribute a lot.

5. A lot of people are having difficulty with "measuring what matters." We might need to ask our business faculty or a consulting group to help us with this.

6. It seems that senior leadership needs to communicate more about what's going on throughout the campus. People want to be more informed about what is taking place more often.

7. We are growing rapidly as a campus. We need to manage this effectively and keep everyone informed, continue to build our capacity, and hire really good people.

Have each group share their recommendations with the whole group and capture this information electronically. Make sure that all the participants get copies of their work.

Senior leaders now have new information they need to review and some recommendations to consider and respond to over time.

IMPLEMENTATION DESIGN 3:
Strategic Plan "Rollout"

One of the biggest challenges facing implementation efforts is the *way* the strategic plan is communicated across the campus. Most folks tend to create some kind of PowerPoint presentation, which is usually way too long and detailed. Then they conduct a series of meetings and walk people through the plan. At the end of the presentation, there might be time for questions and answers but usually the presenters are met with silence.

They continue this process, which could easily take a couple of weeks, until all units and departments have had a chance to attend an in-person presentation. It takes a great deal of time and attention and is woefully inadequate.

I will share with you a rollout process I created for two campuses that greatly improved the communication and, more importantly, the understanding of the strategic plan throughout the campus. We know this because we anonymously assessed each meeting and continued to improve the rollout process as we moved forward.

Steps…

1. We had all the vice presidents meet with the middle managers (assistant VPs, directors, managers) and they shared the draft of the strategic plan. We kept this to a 30-minute presentation so we didn't overwhelm participants with too much detail. The initial group had about 50 participants.

   Then we handed out large index cards and asked people to anonymously write down their questions, concerns, and what they liked about the proposed plan.

   The cards were collected and the vice presidents took turns answering and responding to the questions and comments. When they didn't have a clear answer for a particular question, we captured it on a "Parking Lot" flip chart in full view of everyone. Specific VPs publicly committed to finding out the answers to these unanswered questions within a week and posting the answers on the campus intranet for viewing. This helps build credibility in the process and doesn't allow some tough or uncomfortable questions to just fade away.

The whole meeting took about two hours and the anonymous meeting evaluation indicated that it was an informative and meaningful experience for almost all attendees. We received an 8.7 rating on a 1 to 10 scale for the meeting and shared the evaluations with all the attendees.

2. The same directors and managers reconvened one week later for a "working" breakfast. They were asked if they had any further questions since they had time to think about some new ones. We spent about 20 minutes on a new question and answer session.

3. We then had them meet in their respective vice presidents groups (e.g., finance, student affairs) and asked them to discuss the implications of the plan and their current work. We suggested several focus questions to guide the discussion and create some structure around it. For example:

    -   "What are we currently doing that is clearly aligned with where the strategic plan will take our campus?"

    -   "What real changes can you anticipate as we begin to implement the plan (e.g., roles, how we allocate resources, how we prioritize our work)?"

    -   "What new training and skill development will you need in order to implement the plan?"

    -   "What do we need to stop doing if we are going to be successful at implementing the plan?"

    -   "What's the most attractive or interesting part of the plan?" (It can't be everything!)

4. After each group had 30 minutes to answer the focus questions, we had each group briefly (five minutes) present their findings.

Implementation Note:

Having all vice presidents at both meetings was critical. It communicated that it was important and that they were in full support of the strategic plan.

Conducting the "implications" conversation is an essential element of the implementation process. Unless people understand the implications and possible impacts the new plan presents, they will not understand it. If you don't understand something, you can't implement it effectively

The implications discussion is not an elegant and smooth conversation initially. It is new territory for most people but it makes them think, discuss, even fumble around a little, which is part of the learning journey.

After the presentations were completed, we had an open forum discussion that was robust and energizing. We asked that each VP have at least one more implications discussion with their people back in their offices.

5. After the second discussion back home, we had each manager who attended the original meetings meet with their respective groups and direct reports and conduct the same process with them (e.g., the initial 30 minute presentation with Q&A, an implications discussion with flip charts, and a second follow-up conversation about implication).

    Once again, they anonymously assessed the effectiveness of these meetings and they scored pretty well (a 7.9). Several important themes emerged from the evaluations:

    *   People appreciated the opportunity to understand the plan and, most importantly, the implications for their specific work. For most, this was the first time they had ever participated in a meeting like this.

    *   People were apprehensive about the potential changes they could anticipate with the implementation of the new plan.

- They wanted similar forums to be organized in the future as the plan was being implemented. This way they would be informed about progress.

- Most participants appreciated the creation of anonymous, honest, and tough questions during the meeting and felt that it built credibility into the process.

Lessons Learned

- Watch out for too many PowerPoints covering way too much. The communication vehicle needs to connect with the audience, not just the presenter.

- Working in smaller groups fosters more open conversation. People liked the small group forums.

- Ensuring anonymity initially was critical because it allowed people to ask the "tough" questions.

- The hardest question for almost everyone to answer was the one about what they might have to *stop* doing!

- Having a couple of conversations about the implications really helped people get their minds wrapped around implementing the plan.

Summary

After this rollout process was concluded, each department created a set of action plans that were shared with others across their division and posted on the intranet for viewing.

We created unit scorecards to measure the progress of each unit's action plans and held *quarterly* meetings with each division, facilitated by the vice presidents to review progress toward goals, identify challenges, and conduct problem solving.

IMPLEMENTATION DESIGN 4:
The Implementation "Clinic"

Problems are *inevitable* and can come up everywhere during an implementation process, but they are often covered up because people are reluctant to ask for help, don't want to appear inadequate, or are "stuck" with what they are doing and don't have any solutions going forward.[28] In my experience, campus stakeholders are often reluctant to share problems with each other.

This highly engaging implementation design creates the opportunity to surface the real problems and challenges campus stakeholders are facing and tap the thinking and resources of participants in generating constructive and realistic solutions to tough problems.

This implementation "design" fully engages participants (they work very hard), helps build the problem solving capacity of people, taps the creativity and wisdom of participants, and helps normalize the fact that people are experiencing problems and challenges.

One caution: This design will only work if the campus climate is safe enough to share real life organizational problems. If failure isn't tolerated, if the trust level is low, or if critics rule the day, don't ever use this design.

A senior leader (e.g., EVP, Provost) needs to convene this kind of meeting and fully support its outcomes. This is an essential element with this type of meeting design. Senior level sponsorship creates both the opportunity and safety needed to operationalize this meeting. It also elevates the importance of the meeting. This should not be an ad hoc, informal meeting where participants congregate, share some problems, and hope things work out. You need senior leadership credibility and support to pull off this initial meeting. Once participants have experienced success with it, they often organize their own implementation clinics back in their workplaces. But the first one needs senior level support.

---

28 Adapted with permission from Sanaghan, P & Gabriel, P. A. (2014). *Collaborative Leadership in Action.* HRD Press. This implementation design was originally called the "Trauma Clinic."

Things to think about:

- You will use 24 participants as a working model for this meeting design.
- You will need a large, comfortable room with moveable chairs.
- Have several flip charts with markers.
- A good, credible facilitator is always helpful but not essential.
- This works well with between 12–24 participants.

This meeting assumes that the participants who are invited to the implementation "clinic" are willing to share their real challenges regarding implementation efforts.

Although you can conduct this design with people from the same campus units (department, school, division), it is best utilized with *cross-boundary* units where people from all over the campus are convened for the meeting. This builds the collaborative "capital" of the campus in powerful ways.

Participants should know ahead of time the intended purposes of the meeting and be encouraged to bring their implementation challenges to the meeting.

How to conduct the meeting

1. The senior leader welcomes participants and has everyone *briefly* introduce themselves. (This is especially important with cross-boundary groups that might not know each other.)

2. The senior leader reviews the purpose of the meeting (i.e., to solve real implementation problems and challenges. They also need to set the tone of the meeting by communicating that "we are here to share the challenges and difficulties we are having with our implementation efforts."

3. The facilitator has the participants (24) count off from one to four. This will result in four groups of six members, randomly mixed.

4. When people organize themselves into the smaller groups of six members, each group member is invited to discuss an actual implementation problem they are currently facing. For example:

- There is a breakdown in communication throughout a division, which is causing people stress and confusion.

- People within the unit are not completing the necessary tasks to move toward stated goals.

- People feel overwhelmed with their current workload and can't pay attention to implementing the new strategic plan.

- There is open conflict between two working groups within the division.

- People are working hard but little is getting accomplished.

- People are confused about who makes what decisions and things are slowing down dramatically.

- A new leader in the division is finding it difficult to get his people on board with implementation efforts.

- People are complaining that measuring progress with too many reports is getting in the way of doing things.

Give them about 20 minutes for this part of the meeting, approximately three minutes per person.

5. After all participants have shared the real implementation challenge, have them select **one** challenge to share with the larger group. This selected problem should be fairly challenging (but not impossible) and actually be "solvable." For example, you wouldn't try and solve a poor campus climate or low campus morale issue with this design. But you could address any of the examples above.

You also don't want to deal with intense personnel issues, like a leader who is a functional alcoholic. That belongs with Human Resources.

6. Each group should then share their implementation challenge with the larger group. Everyone should hear all four selected challenges.

7. Before the reporting out, the facilitator should inform partic-
    ipants that "we are going to act as consultants to each other."
    Each group will "inherit" one of the implementation challenges
    from another group and then act as consultants to that group.

For example: A   B   C   D

-   Group B acts as a consultant to Group A.
-   Group C acts as a consultant to Group B.
-   Group D acts as a consultant to Group C.
-   Group A acts as a consultant to Group D.

Strategic note: Having another group "inherit" the implementation
challenge of another group is a key element in this meeting design.
Often, we get stuck with a problem or challenge and can't envision
alternatives or possibilities. Having someone else inherit the problem creates psychological distance and the opportunity for new and
fresh perspectives and ideas to be created.

This is one of the most important ideas I have encountered in my
consulting. We all have blind spots. This has nothing to do with
intelligence. It's just the way it is. *Everyone* has blind spots, even organizations such as Nokia, which had a billion customers at one time
and didn't see that Apple was coming at them.

The good news is that we can reduce our blind spots by asking others
for help. When someone with a different perspective, background,
gender, race etc., is invited, they will see things we simply cannot see.
That's the blessing of authentic collaborative work, where different,
cross-boundary groups work together. "We" can then see the whole
and reveal the hidden parts.

Implementation Note:

Readers who are interested in understanding more about blind spots
will find Max Bazerman and Ann Tenbrunsel's book, *Blind Spots*,
helpful.[29]

---

29 Bazerman, M. H. & Tenbrunsel, A. E. (2011). *Blind Spots: Why We Fail to Do What's
Right and What to Do About It*. Princeton University Press.

8. After everyone hears the four challenging implementation problems (one from each group) and inherits another group's problem, each "consulting" group should be given 10 minutes to come up with four or five "diagnostic" questions that will enable them to better understand their inherited problem before they jump to quick solutions.

These questions should be mostly open-ended and create new information rather than simple yes or no questions. The goal here is for each "consulting" group to better understand the complexity of the other's situation.

It is helpful to have a group member be a recorder and capture the diagnostic questions.

For example:

- "How long has this implementation challenge existed?" "How has it been handled so far? Please give examples."

- "What would success look like to you? What measures do you want to see?"

- "What do you think needs to change to help move things forward?"

- "Describe the culture of the division. A brief story or two that represents the culture would be helpful."

- "How can senior leadership help with this challenge? Do they know it exists?"

- "What is the one thing, in your view, that if changed would have a positive impact on the problem?"

9. After each consulting group has had 10 minutes to create their diagnostic questions, each group should then be given the opportunity to ask their consulting questions. Take one challenge at a time and have each consulting group ask their questions.

This will be very interesting for participants because they will hear some great diagnostic questions (which they tend to remember) and they learn about the complexity of the challenges their colleagues face.

Implementation Note:

Limit the number of questions to five for each consulting group because if there are too many questions, the meeting will drag along.

As participants ask their five questions and receive new information, there will be a tendency to ask a lot of follow-up questions. The facilitator needs to be fairly strict about this; watch out for the number of questions asked or this will drag on.

10. After the questions have all been asked and answered, take a 10-minute stretch break. You want to avoid information overload, and it is also helpful to "step away" and create some psychological distance before the consulting groups create solutions.

    At this stage in the meeting, participants have accomplished several things:

    a. Discussed real implementation challenges with everyone.

    b. Selected one challenge to solve.

    c. Created a set of diagnostic questions to be more fully informed.

    d. Had an opportunity to ask questions and be more fully informed before suggesting solutions.

    When the participants return from the break, the facilitator can allow each group the opportunity to ask *one* follow-up question. Often, participants have a new insight they want to explore and this gives them a last shot at their inherited challenge.

11. Then once each consulting group has asked their bonus question, each group is given 15 minutes to come up with ideas on how to solve their consulting problem. Their goal is to act as consultants and provide high quality, creative, practical ideas for their client.

12. At this stage, each consulting group takes a turn sharing their advice and ideas about their client's problem. After the consulting group provides its ideas, the facilitator can open up the floor and ask the larger group if they have any additional advice or insights into the focus problem. Limit this to a couple of minutes and go on to the next challenge.

13. After the final round, the facilitator or senior leader can have the participants discuss their reactions to the implementation clinic. Keep this to about 10 minutes.

It is always helpful to *anonymously* evaluate participants' reactions to the implementation clinic. This is a *very different* approach to organizational problem solving and it is important to understand how people experience it.

Publish the anonymous results quickly so participants can see what others thought about this kind of meeting. Almost always, participants find the meeting value added and want to continue this kind of meeting on a regular basis.

***

Implementation Note:

I have worked with two campuses that utilize this problem solving design on a regular basis. With one campus, they have a monthly "Chat and Chew" with a cross-boundary group of 20 directors. They meet over lunch, have a little food and conversation, and then walk through the design steps.

***

They have been doing this for over five years. Attendance is stellar because the meeting really works for them. Each "clinic" is anonymously evaluated and the feedback goes to all the participants and their direct supervisors. This builds in accountability for the time invested.

The second campus does a quarterly Implementation Clinic and follows generally the same process, including evaluations. They are considering creating one at the VP level—we will see if that emerges. In my experience, the higher up you go in the hierarchy, the more reluctant senior type leaders are willing to share their challenges with others. This should change given the COVID-19 world we now live in. We will need to more fully involve others and seek multiple perspectives if we are to deal effectively with the pace of change and the complexity higher education now faces. I think that senior leaders are often reluctant to say that they don't know something or to ask for help. I have seen this play out on the campuses of large and famous universities who were "bold" when they said they would have on campus experiences for their students in the fall of 2020 and now they are quickly retreating to Plans B and C.

IMPLEMENTATION DESIGN 5:
The Stakeholder Review

This simple and informative design comes from my colleague, Dr. Nancy Aronson, who cocreated the *System Coherence Framework* that enables organizations to deeply understand how to create holistic approaches to planning, thinking, and action planning. What makes it so effective is that it identifies specific individuals and groups within the campus and external to the campus that you will need support from with your implementation efforts.

Three key aspects of the system are:

1. It highlights what is needed from these individuals and groups (e.g., information, resources, specific actions, deep expertise, political support).

2. It helps identify what their interests might be in helping you with your implementation efforts. "What is in it for them?" WIIFT is an essential question to ask when working with other groups. You can talk about collegiality and helping with the common good all day long but if you cannot determine their specific interests, your ability to enroll them will be very limited.

3. Lastly, it asks you to identify what you believe is their current level of support and commitment on a scale from one (low) to five (high).

Although individual leaders could fill out the stakeholder review, it is best conducted with a large, diverse work group or team (10–20 participants). Prior to the meeting, the list of questions like the ones below needs to be sent out and ask participants to think about their answers to the questions. You want them mentally prepared to get into the heart of the meeting quickly. These stakeholder elements will help people think about who can help with your implementation efforts:

Identify who are the "stakeholders" (groups or people) by analyzing these factors:

- Who is important to the success of your initiative or plans.
- Who has strategic *information.*
- Who can give you good *advice.*
- Who has access to *resources* you might need.
- Who has to *implement* or *take action* in support of your efforts.
- Who will be *impacted* by your efforts.
- Who has to be *willing to own* this to make it happen.
- Who has the *authority* to move things along.
- Who can *block* or *help* your efforts politically.

Open up the meeting with a clarifying purpose statement like, "We are here today to identify those people and groups we need to enroll in our implementation efforts. (This could be with your strategic planning efforts or special initiatives.)

Walk through the focus questions. What is needed from them? What do you know about their interests (WIIFT). It is helpful to provide a working example of what you are looking for. For example:

1. **PERSON/GROUP**

   FACULTY SENATE

2. **WHAT DO WE NEED FROM THEM?**

WE NEED THEIR STRONG PARTICIPATION ON OUR PLANNING TASK FORCES GOING FORWARD

3. **WHAT IS THEIR CURRENT LEVEL OF INTEREST OR SUPPORT? (SCALE= 1–5)**

About a "2"

4. **WHAT IS IN IT FOR THEM TO HELP US?**

ENSURE THAT THE FACULTY VOICE IS HEARD THROUGHOUT THE IMPLEMENTATION PROCESS.

THEY CAN HELP SHAPE THE IMPLEMENTATION AGENDA AND GET THINGS DONE THAT ARE IMPORTANT TO THEM.

THEY CAN HELP CREATE THE ACADEMIC PLAN AND SUPPORT THEIR RESEARCH INTERESTS.

5. **HOW CAN WE HELP THEM?**

WE CAN INCREASE FOCUSED RESOURCES ($$$; TEACHING ASSISTANTS; PROFESSIONAL DEVELOPMENT; UNIVERSITY PRESS PUBLISHING) TO ENHANCE THEIR RESEARCH AGENDA.

6. **WHO IS THE APPROPRIATE CONTACT?**

THE PROVOST

After walking through the working example, give people about 15 minutes to fill in their information on the wall chart. This part doesn't need to be orchestrated or tightly organized but some people might want a little more structure when filling in the chart; it's your call.

I would suggest that when you get to the scoring part about the level of support (from 1–5), you make sure that participants' scores are *anonymous* to ensure honest answers. You can do this by using Post-it notes and have people assign their numbers and put them on the wall in the appropriate space.

I realize that giving a score (1–5) for the *perceived* level of support is less rigorous than some might want. I use common sense with this part because it's an important score to understand. If you have 20 people in the room and the score is a 2.1 for support, you probably have a lot of work to do. On the other hand, if you get a 4.3 average, you probably have some chance at success.

In a relatively short period of time, you will have an informal "snapshot" of those stakeholders that can help you with your implementation efforts. This might well be the first time people have seen a "map" like this. I have found that it shows folks that there is almost always lots of potential support for their implementation efforts. This is very encouraging for them.

This "snapshot" needs to be captured electronically and distributed to participants as a record of their work and thinking. A small group of four to five campus leaders then needs to spend some time organizing this information so that it can be acted on.

IMPLEMENTATION DESIGN 6:
Creating an Adhocracy Map

Earlier, I discussed the important role of credible *informal* leaders, or the adhocracy, on a campus. These are the go-to people who get "stuff done." They are invaluable to implementation efforts. For those individuals who are interested in learning more about these individuals, I would suggest reading three helpful articles:

1. Rob Cross and Lawrence Prusak, "The People Who Make Organizations Go—or Stop," *Harvard Business Review* (June 2002). https://hbr.org/2002/06/the-people-who-make-organizations-go-or-stop

2. Lowell L. Bryan, Eric Matson, and Leigh M. Weiss, "Harnessing the Power of Informal Employee Networks," *McKinsey Quarterly* (November 1, 2007). https://www.mckinsey.com/business-functions/organization/our-insights/harnessing-the-power-of-informal-employee-networks#

3. Rob Cross, Peter Gray, Shirley Cunningham, Mark Showers, and Robert J. Thomas, "The Collaborative Organization: How to Make Employee Networks Really Work," *MIT Sloan Management Review* (October 1, 2010). https://sloanreview.mit.edu/article/the-collaborative-organization-how-to-make-employee-networks-really-work/

Although they do not specifically address implementation efforts, they add valuable ideas and insights on how to identify and enroll these individuals in your organizational efforts. I describe two of these articles briefly in the Annotated Bibliography section of the book.

This large group meeting design will help you identify these individuals across the campus and, more importantly, enroll them in your implementation efforts.

Senior leadership would convene a group of all their immediate direct reports and also include all their direct reporters' direct reports. This easily could be a group of 30–50 leaders. Do not be concerned about the size of this group—the meeting "design" is easy to organize and delivers great results in a short period of time.

The senior leaders would foreshadow that the purpose of the meeting is to identify those individuals who work in their departments, work units, and divisions, and who work hard every day to advance the campus' goals and objectives. (This can't be *everybody*!) These are the ones who go above and beyond the call of duty most of the time and are seen by others as "go-to" people.

Some of these are well known; others will be unsung heroes. Let the participants know that leaders across the campus will be convened to create a "Talent Bank" of these important contributors, and the results will be shared with everyone who attends the meeting. A set of focus questions (see below) should be sent to all the participants prior to the meeting so that they can prepare their answers ahead of time.

Implementation Note:

Some people might read this and ask, "Why don't you just have people create a list, send it in electronically, and compile it for distribution?" This would be an "efficient" approach but, unfortunately, it is *not* an effective one. One of the most important notions you can take away from this book is the importance of "relational capital." It is the fuel of the implementation engine.

It is what gets things done. Not charts, or technology, or money, or even great ideas. It is through people that things get accomplished. Of course, this is common sense, but the key thing to always remember is that it is the relationships that are developed during the implementation process that get things done. So as an "Implementation Champion," one needs to ask, "How do I continue to build and nurture the relational capital on my campus?"

This might be *the one big takeaway* from all my planning experience: It's not great ideas or effective planning that ensures success. Strangely, this relational "stuff" isn't talked about much in the implementation literature but for my money it is "the" factor for successful implementation. In the many planning projects I have done over the years, I have found that "relational capital" (e.g., the trust between faculty and administrators, authentic staff engagement) is the key to success; if it is present, good things can happen, when it isn't, good luck.

Almost all the meeting designs and practices in this book pay attention to the relational part of planning (e.g., authentic engagement, transparency, inclusion, seeking multiple perspectives, and hearing all the voices).

We have fallen victim to a whole range of "technologies" (e.g., Gantt charts, Critical Path Method, Dependency Charts) that make planning and implementation "efficient." But the problem is, not much actually gets done. People are busy, for sure, but they're working in silos, sending in reports, creating fancy charts for others to review;

real learning and sharing doesn't take place. And by the way, who reads all those reports?

Anytime you can get people together to accomplish a real task, share ideas and best practices, and problem solve together, please take advantage of it. It is the missing link regarding implementation. When people build authentic relationships, get to know each other a little, help each other out in service of something meaningful like the campus strategic plan, you will see powerful implementation taking place over time. Relational capital is essential to implementation and execution. Never forget this.

On a wall, a large matrix with flip chart paper (approximately 40 feet long) would be created that includes these descriptors:

CAREER TECH

INDIVIDUAL	CURRENT ROLE	LOCATION (DEPT./DIVISION)	WHAT ARE THEIR SKILLS & QUALITIES	
JOE	Executive Assistant	Academic Affairs	• E.Q. Collaborative • Follow-up • Intelligence	• Moral Compass • Great communication style
PAUL	Executive Assistant	Administration	• Quiet Competence • Organizational skills	• Institutional knowledge & history
CHRISTINE	CLA-Welding Machinery	Welding	• Student focus • ATC grad	• Hard working • Dedicated
BRIDGET	CT Rep	PWT	• Go-getter • Task-focused • Hard-worker	• Dedicated
MARY	Dean — Academics	Academic Affairs	• Relationship-based • Collaborative	• Great at developing partnerships

INDIVIDUAL	ANY PROJECTS THEY HAVE IMPLEMENTED	DIRECT SUPERVISOR	PERSON RECOMMENDING
JOE	Academic initiatives — too many too mention	Mary	Todd
PAUL	HLC, FSGC support, Foundation (not large, project-based)	Mary	Derrick
CHRISTINE	Strategic Planning, K-12 initatives	Mary	Cheryl Heidi
BRIDGET	Variety of tasks	Steve	Steve
MARY	Major donations	Bill	Bill

CAREER TECH
BRANCH CAMPUS 2

INDIVIDUAL	CURRENT ROLE	LOCATION (DEPT./DIVISION)	WHAT ARE THEIR SKILLS & QUALITIES
DAN	Lab Supervisor	Science/CC & CR	• Organization • Logistics • Planning
ABBIE	Admission & Academic Supervisor	Student Services	• Organized • Hard worker • Leader
MARTHA	Biology Faculty	CC Faculty	• Collaborator • Logistics • Details • Outreach
DIANE	CE/CT Rep	PWT	• Community connections • Project management
KEN	IT Pro	IT CC/ATC	• Always willing to push change
JON	IT Pro	IT CC/ATC	• Always willing to push change
BETH	Psychology Faculty	CC	• Organized • Committed • Thoughtful
ERICA	PT Languages FYE Faculty	CC	• Collaboration • Student success

INDIVIDUAL	ANY PROJECTS THEY HAVE IMPLEMENTED	DIRECT SUPERVISOR	PERSON RECOMMENDING
DAN	Staff Development	Nicole	Casey
ABBIE	PSEO, Accuplacer in H.S., H.S. concerns	Ashley	Ashley
MARY	Faculty Development	Nicole	Andy
DIANE	Non-credit CAN @ Grace Point	Dan	Andy
KEN	Tech upgrades	Kevin	Kevin Andy
JON	Tech upgrades	Kevin	Kevin Andy
BETH	State-Level BOT	Erin	Mary
ERICA	FYE	Joe	Andy

INDIVIDUAL

THEIR CURRENT ROLE AND LOCATION (dept., division, school)

WHAT ARE THEIR SKILLS AND QUALITIES? (what gifts do they bring to the table?)

WHAT IS THEIR CONTACT INFORMATION?

WHAT ARE TWO IMPLEMENTATION PROJECTS THEY HELPED COMPLETE OVER THE PAST ONE TO THREE YEARS? (This is the "reality check" for the whole design. You want people nominated who have actually accomplished some important things, not a popularity contest.)

WHO IS THEIR DIRECT SUPERVISOR? (so we can contact them)

WHAT IS YOUR RELATIONSHIP WITH THEM? (e.g., colleague, direct report, peer, friend)

Participants would use large Post-its (at least 3 x 5 inches) and fill in the answers to the set of focus questions by putting the Post-its right on the wall.

This will only take about 15 minutes to create and will generate a lot of interest and enthusiasm for participants. In a short period of time, you will have a wall full of great implementation information.

A couple of things should happen next…

A. Have participants work in small, (five to six people) cross-boundary groups that represent the different functional silos on campus (e.g., finance, student development, athletics) and review the information together. Give them a set of focus questions to help structure their review process. For example:

1. What surprises did you encounter?

    - A project you knew nothing about.
    - The name of a person you never heard about.

2. What are some of the strong themes about skills and qualities that are present?

3. Are there opportunities for cross-divisional training where people with certain skills can help leverage efforts elsewhere?

4. Are there completed projects that might make a best case study? Ones that we can learn from?

5. Are there certain supervisors that tend to develop their people or have several of these "doers?"

Give them about 15 minutes to capture their thinking and answers for the focus questions. Make sure that there is a recorder in each group. Then have each group create a brief report out about what they found in the review process. Have someone capture this information in an electronic format.

Let people know that all this information will be captured electronically and sent to them in a short period of time. Encourage them to share this information with those individuals who are on the wall chart. It is nice to be acknowledged for your contribution to campus.

As mentioned earlier in the book, this adhocracy implementation group should be convened a couple of times a year by the senior leadership to assess implementation progress, identify real challenges going forward, and problem solve implementation issues. This will create a powerful network of people who will move the plan forward. Pay attention to this group.

For some campuses, this could be a rather large group of people to convene. If that's the case for a particular campus, then have smaller gatherings of 30–40 people instead of 100 plus. The key thing to remember is this: Make sure you have cross-boundary representation with any group you convene. Do not do it by school or division, that keeps the conversations in the institutional silos; make sure that cross-boundary groups are convened, that way you build the network that you will need to implement the plan. It also will build the cross-boundary relational capital that is so important to implementation efforts.

Lastly, one of the great frustrations that senior leaders have about their campus is this: They know many (not all) of the good things that are happening on campus. Unfortunately, many people are unaware of these great accomplishments and successes. This is not good. The corporate sector learned a long time ago how important it is to acknowledge successes and accomplishments and share these widely. We can learn a lot from their efforts. People can't leverage their efforts if they don't know what others are doing. This kind of meeting can be a beginning effort to ensure that "more people know more" about what's going on throughout the institution.

It takes an hour or so and will provide great information. And remember to have some food at the meeting!

IMPLEMENTATION DESIGN 6:
The Interview Design

This meeting design, created by Dr. Rodney Napier, a former colleague and business partner, is one of the most powerful, collaborative, and engaging meeting designs around. It will change the way people think about collaborative planning and implementation because it is interactive, focused, interesting, and outcome-based all at the same time. It can be utilized with large groups of 50, 75, even 100 participants and it can be completed in a relatively modest amount of time.

It is impressive to see a large group of 50–100 people working together collaboratively, openly sharing ideas and information, and creating prioritized and strategic information in about 2–2½ hours. The data obtained from the meeting is undeniable because it is collected with everyone's input and in full view of everyone. People appreciate the transparency of this design and tend to trust the data that they collaboratively create.

This design can create a somewhat difficult logistical challenge because you will need a large room, since participants will be moving around quite a bit. It takes some planning up front to be successful, but it is well worth the effort.

On many of the campuses I have worked with, on average, we have meaningfully engaged over 1,000 people in the strategic planning process. This type of design will show the reader *how* you can collectively engage large numbers of people in thinking about the future of their campus and creating the implementation strategies to achieve your goals.

(We will use 50 participants as a model for this design.)

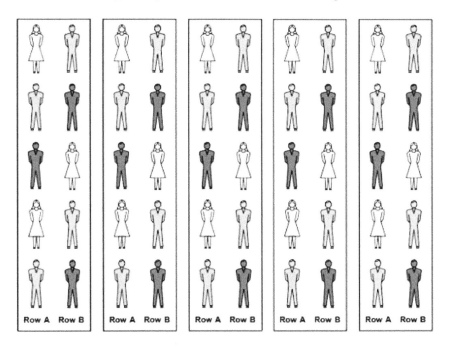

The room should be arranged in pairs of rows facing each other. In our working example, we have five planning and implementation questions.

It will enable planning leaders to engage as many stakeholders as they want. The goal here is not to just accumulate big numbers of engaged stakeholders to impress people but when you have created a stakeholder database that has been sourced from hundreds, if not thousands of people, it has power.

The following are some examples of strategic questions we have asked on campuses. You will see that you can ask almost any question and it will provide the planning group with very honest, coherent information about the questions asked. Make sure you are ready for the answers!

1. "What is the main reason we are not yet a stellar institution?"

2. "What are you most proud of about this university?"

3. "How can we further improve campus-wide communication?"

4. "What implementation challenges do you anticipate us needing to deal with effectively over the next two to three years?"

5. "What is one piece of advice you would like to give to the president and to the trustees as we start implementing our plans? Explain your answer."

6. "What institutional values must we preserve at all costs?"

7. "What can we do to improve diversity on this campus?"

8. "What is a best practice that you know about that would help us improve our implementation efforts?"

9. "What key issues must we deal with if we are to achieve excellence as an institution?"

10. "What is one thing we must change (e.g., do more of, less of, get rid of) if we are to be successful in the near future (one to three years)?"

11. "How would you describe campus culture?"

12. "What are some things you enjoy about student life on campus? What don't you enjoy about student life?"

13. "What about our history helps us as an institution? Hinders us? Hurts us?"

14. "What are our lived institutional "values" that inform and govern our behavior?"

15. "What is the biggest implementation challenge you see that will prevent us from going forward?"

As you can see, you can ask a variety of engaging and strategic questions. You want to make sure that you send the questions to participants prior to the meeting so that they have some thinking time for their answers.

For this working example, we will utilize the following five focus questions to show how the design works.

1. "If you were talking with a colleague about Incredible University, how would you describe it?"

2. "What must senior leadership (e.g., the president and cabinet) do to ensure the successful implementation of the strategic planning process?"

3. "How should we communicate how we are doing regarding the implementation of our plan (e.g., a campus scorecard, town hall meetings, quarterly reports)?"

4. "What are some important challenges that you see with the effective implementation of our strategic plan?"

5. "What are some important questions we need to ask our campus stakeholders about Incredible University?"

Helpful Hint:

It is important to stagger the questions in Row B so that when you begin the process, participants are not asking the same question of each other.

The Facilitator's Directions

1. The participants in Row A will start the interview process. They will ask their "partner," the person sitting across from them, their focus question and record their partner's responses, *unedited* for two minutes. (It is important to emphasize the unedited part because this is a data gathering meeting design. You don't want

people deciding on their own whether to include a participant's responses or not.)

Helpful Hints:

People in Row B, who move, should remember to bring their question with them.

If you have "extra" people (e.g., 52 people instead of 50) put them on the end of one of the Row A, the row that does not move.

2. The participants in Row B will then ask their partner their focus question and record their unedited responses for two minutes.

3. After Rows A and B have asked and answered their question, that is the end of a "round." People in Row B move down one seat and one person at the end of Row B rotates up to the first seat in the row.

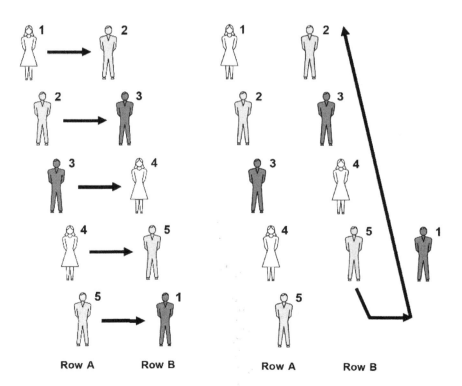

| Row A | Row B | Row A | Row B |

4. Each participant will have a new partner with a new question and the original process continues (e.g., Row A asks their question and records their partner's responses unedited for two minutes). Then Row B asks their question and records their partner's responses unedited.

You will continue the rotating seats until all the questions have been asked and answered. At the end of approximately 30 minutes, every person will have been interviewed five times and they will have interviewed five people.

Second Half of the Meeting

After the initial data gathering/interviewing process, have participants sit quietly for 10 minutes by themselves and organize their interview data into one of the following three categories:

Truths: These are the responses or answers expressed by almost every person they interviewed. They are very strong ideas—they "leap" off the page. (You may find that participants don't have any "truths" and this is okay.)

Trends: Those responses given by two or three people. It is not as strong as a "truth" but more than one person provided the answer.

Unique Ideas: These are individual ideas that represent a different, creative, unique perspective or idea. It is *not* a laundry list of every idea that was shared. Each person must judge for themselves if there is a "unique" idea in their interview data that should be part of the database. Once again, participants might easily find that they do not have a *unique* idea in the interview data.

After individuals have organized their interview data into the three categories, have them join with the others who have the same question. In our working model of five questions, you would have five stations and have 10 participants at each station.

The main reason you have participants organize their data individually is to ensure that when they move into the larger question groups in the next step of the process, they are well prepared for the discussion.

Instruct the participants to use self-managed roles (facilitator, recorder, time keeper, presenter) and take 45 minutes to pool their group information regarding their focus question and put the truths, trends, and unique ideas for their focus question on flipchart paper.

After the five focus question groups have created their truths, trends, and unique ideas for their question, have each group present their findings to the larger group.

The presentations should only take three to five minutes each.

After the presentations, the facilitator can lead a brief discussion about participants' reactions to the shared information. Keep this to 10–15 minutes.

Once again, let participants know that their data will be shared with everyone in the room as soon as possible.

Here are two examples of the answers to the focus question data from our original five questions:

1. What must senior leadership (i.e., president and the cabinet) do to ensure the successful implementation of the strategic planning process?

    Truths

    - They must be visible and engaged throughout the process.
    - They must listen to people.
    - They must share all the information we gather with campus stakeholders (be transparent).
    - They must be visibly committed to implementing the strategic planning process.

Trends

- Have regular campus breakfast meetings to keep people informed about the process.
- The president should include updates about the planning process in her weekly letter to the campus.
- Let us know how the planning decisions will be made.
- Be transparent with the budget.

Unique Ideas

- Ask the mayor to participate in the planning task force.
- Identify faculty who have expertise in strategic planning and use them as a reality check throughout the process.

2. What are some important questions we need to ask our campus stakeholders about Incredible University?

Truths

- What are the strengths of Incredible University? What do you feel most proud about?
- What are some challenges facing this university over the next 5–10 years?
- What two changes or improvements would you make with the physical plant/infrastructure of the campus?
- What are the most important trends and issues we need to pay attention to as we plan for the future?
- How would you describe the culture of Incredible University? (Open, welcoming, critical, not sure, etc.)
- How can we improve the quality of student life on campus?
- How would you describe the quality of our faculty's teaching in the classroom?

Trends

- What are some areas we need to improve as an institution? (Be specific.)

- What is one piece of advice you would like to give to the president that would enable her to lead even more effectively?
- What keeps us from being great at everything we do?
- When you talk about Incredible University to your family and friends, what do you say?
- How can we use technology to improve the educational experience in the classroom? Elsewhere?
- How can we further improve campus communication?

Unique Ideas

- What difficult issue do we need to openly discuss that currently is avoided? How can we further improve collaboration across campus?

IMPLEMENTATION DESIGN 7:
Opportunity Mapping

This is an adaptation of a planning tool, sometimes called the "Solutions Matrix" that I have utilized with campus leaders to *anonymously* assess the potential benefits of a proposed idea. It can be used to assess a potential initiative, a strategic partnership, or a new idea the president or senior leader really likes.

It provides some objectivity and rigor for the decision-making process and is especially useful *before* a decision is made. Boards have also found this to be a useful protocol to utilize to inform their discussions and decision-making.It's a very strategic protocol to use because there aren't enough resources to implement all the things we want to accomplish. Many people in higher education are quite aspirational and want to do more to enhance the educational experience, improve the student experience, elevate faculty scholarship, and the reputation and brand of the campus. These are all good ideas, but we need to not "fall in love" with too many ideas or be persuaded by strong voices or political power.

Briefly, a set of agreed upon criteria is used to visually depict how decision makers "see" an opportunity. It is critical that the scoring of the criteria is *anonymous* to ensure honest responses and to make sure that one person's scores (e.g., the president, provost, board chair) doesn't overly influence the grading of the criteria. Once the scores are plotted, a great database for discussion is created.

The following example is from a senior cabinet that is assessing a strategic alliance with an online education company. The president is *very excited* about this opportunity and wants to close the deal soon. The Provost suggested that they use this decision support process because they had used it successfully with their deans and thought it would provide some rigor to the decision process.

When a decision maker doesn't have an answer for a particular criteria, they put in a question mark rather than leaving it blank. More than a few question marks would indicate that the decision makers need more information before they can make a good decision.

	1	2	3	4	5
We know this company well.	*		**	**	*
We trust their reputation.	??	*	**		*
They have excellent experience in higher education.		***	**		*
This will help make us more competitive.		**	**	*	*
The potential payoff is worth the effort and the money.	*	**		**	*
This will increase profit margin.	*	*	***		*
It will increase our attractiveness to students.		*	**	**	*

Scoring criteria

1 = Poor   2 = Fair   3 = Good   4 = Very Good   5 = Excellent

It is easy to see that this decision has a couple of areas of real concern. Although the scores are anonymous, one decision maker (probably the president) clearly sees this opportunity dramatically different than the others. Several people simply don't have an answer for two of the important criteria (trust and reputation) and further investigation seems warranted.

The visual depiction of the scores will create a robust opportunity for the discussion. Obviously, the president can override the decision but they do so with some peril involved. If really smart cabinet members simply do not think this is a good idea, implementation will be difficult.

Earlier in the book, I talked about the president who had 31 "hidden" initiatives, which deeply impacted implementation efforts because there was simply too much for people to do and they were exhausted. Using a simple process like "Opportunity Mapping" will help prioritize all the wonderful ideas that seem to be all over the place. Focusing on only those ideas that meet the high standards established will help greatly with implementation efforts. Resources are always limited so focusing on the truly important is essential.

This protocol can be used at multiple levels (e.g., board, senior cabinet, departments) and encourages input from others, neutralizes the impact of "powerful" personalities, which we highlighted earlier in the book, and it creates a shared and transparent database. The campus clients who have utilized this practice report that they find it very useful.

IMPLEMENTATION DESIGN 8:
The Future Timeline[30]

This meeting design enables groups both small (10 people) and large (100-plus people) to anticipate the future events, trends, and issues that could potentially impact or influence their organization over the next five to 10 years. It is a highly interactive, interesting, and

---

30 This future-thinking design was first published by NACUBO in my book: Sanaghan, P. *Collaborative Strategic Planning*. It is used with permission.

informative design that encourages people to look outward at external realities and create possible future scenarios. Its primary goal is to create a powerful database for informed strategic thinking, anticipatory thinking, environmental scanning, and sense making.

Number of Participants: 15–100

The Activity:

1. Using 48 participants as the example, tape 10 sheets of flip chart paper to the wall—one sheet per year for the next 10 years. (If participants number 60 or more, use two Future Timelines and two facilitators.)

The room should look like this:

2. Give each participant 10 Post-it notes (3 x 5 inches is best).

3. Instruct participants as follows: "Please think about the future events, trends, and issues that could impact or influence (either positively or negatively) the way Incredible University provides its services, conducts its business, or operates over the next five to 10 years.

Provide several definitions on a flip chart or handout. For example:

- An **event** is a single occurrence. (Examples include: regulatory legislation, retirement of the System Chancellor, new president, a big gift from a donor, new governor.)

- An **issue** is an important theme with substantial power and influence to impact a company. (Examples include: adjunct faculty compensation, diversity and inclusion, retention, the intense focus on job related skills, questioning the value of a degree.)

- A **trend** is an ongoing set of circumstances that has consistency and momentum. (Examples include: dramatically changing demographics, aging faculty, increased global competition, foreign students not coming to the US.)

4. After reviewing the definitions and checking for understanding, provide the following instructions:

   - Write down one event, trend, or issue per Post-it.

   - Indicate if a trend or issue will last for a while.

   - Because we will review the Post-it notes in a few minutes, legibility is important!

   - When you are ready, go to the Future Timeline and populate it by placing your events, trends, and issues in the years you believe they will occur.

   - If you see a Post-it note on the Timeline that is similar to yours, please check it to indicate agreement and discard your Post-it. This reduces redundancies, keeps the Timeline from becoming too cluttered, and captures everyone's information.

5. Give participants about 10–12 minutes to think and write on the Post-it notes and populate the Future Timeline. This generates a tremendous amount of information for participants to distill and understand very quickly.

6. Ask participants to create small, mixed groups of four. Participants can self-organize or use a counting off method of one to 12, to produce 12 groups of four participants each.

7. Instruct the participants as follows: "Please work with your group of four and review the Post-it notes on the timeline. Your goal in the next 15 minutes is to search through all the information and generally agree on the three most important issues, events or trends—not three per category, but *three in total*, that Incredible University must manage effectively if it is to thrive in the future."

   Instruct the group to identify, if they can, a "surprise" or "discovery" from the Post-it notes. This is when they see an event, trend, or issue they didn't expect to see, sometimes these unanticipated "blips" can become important challenges down the road.

8. After the small groups have reviewed the Future Timeline and agreed on their top three issues, events, and trends, create a master list on flip chart paper in full view of everyone. Using the round-robin approach, take one idea from each group until all the ideas are captured. Check off similar ideas to begin prioritizing the list.

Typically, your master list will contain between 10 and 15 prioritized themes. Your list might look like the one below:

Issues, Events, and Trends

- There is a dramatic decrease in foreign students coming to our campus.
- Technology costs will only increase due to the strong demand for cutting-edge technology by our students.
- Our health care costs will continue to skyrocket.
- Our online courses need a dramatic overhaul to be relevant to today's learner.
- Our state legislators are unfriendly to higher education, and we cannot expect their support going forward.
- Regional competition will greatly increase.
- The pool of graduating high school students is dropping fast.
- Many of our leaders and faculty will retire over the next five years.

Surprises and Discoveries

1. Parents of our undergraduate students are fine with certificates and badges and are dramatically rethinking the need for a degree.

2. Preparation for leadership, both administrative and academic, is not on our current radar screen. We have no bench and we need one quickly!

3. The defunding of public higher education will only increase over the next five years.

CHAPTER 4

Team Implementation

This chapter contains several practices and protocols that are effective in building the implementation capacity of teams and work groups. In the end, it's these people who actually accomplish things and are essential to implementation success. They are:

1. Creating Delegation Maps

2. Conducting an After Action Review

3. The Team Alignment Process

4. The Supervisory Dialogue

5. The Meeting Evaluation Survey

6. The Decision Rules

TEAM PROTOCOL 1:
Use "Delegation Maps" to Handle Increased Workload

Most people on campus have full-time jobs and a big workload. The plate is only so large and can only hold so much work, but often it gets piled higher and higher with new tasks and responsibilities. Because most folks are deeply dedicated to the mission of the campus, they take on far more than they should. Over time, mistakes are made, key work slips between the cracks, and people burn out. When a new strategic plan is created, it means that a lot of "new stuff" will need to be done. The essential question then is: what do you do with the stuff that is already on staff's plates?

This is one of the crushing dilemmas facing successful implementation. Unless people can move things off their current plate to make room for the "new stuff," implementation will falter. This is true for the president's senior cabinet all the way down to frontline managers.

Leaders also need to understand that many of their people need training on *how* to prioritize their work so that they can focus on doing the most important work with the bulk of their time. People are put in a terrible bind when new tasks are assigned to their already full plate. Unless they can get rid of low priority tasks, delegate some work to others, or simply quit doing some non-value added activities, they will not be able to create the space and time needed to do more strategic or new work.

This might sound simple but it is one of the most powerful notions regarding implementation. Leaders need to create "delegation maps" with all their direct reports and help prioritize their work into one of three buckets:

1. **Bucket A:** These are essential tasks and assignments that are critical to achieving meaningful results. It is at the heart of what a person is responsible for and cannot be delegated to others. The key to remember with this bucket is that it represents somewhere between 50–60 percent of a person's current responsibilities—*not 95 percent of them.*

    For example, these would be strategic planning meetings that you chair weekly with your senior team, contract discussions with the union leaders, important customer interface marketing decisions, resource allocation meetings, and fundraising.

2. **Bucket B:** These are primarily activities that could be prudently delegated to someone else (and not just dumped on them). With some coaching and support, these responsibilities could be given to a competent person over time. This delegation of responsibil-

ities should develop the capacity of the person who is assigned these activities or they will resent the assignment. This bucket represents between 15–20 percent of a person's current responsibilities. When work is delegated well *over time*, it can free up a considerable amount of time for leaders to focus on the most important work.

For example, a "regular" meeting you traditionally attend that isn't a good use of your time and that a trusted direct report could take responsibility for quickly. Also, it could be a budget report that takes some real time and plays to your strengths as a finance person but someone on your team could be trained to execute it and save you time.

3. **Bucket C:** These are nonessential tasks and low priority activities that we tend to hold onto but are not value-added. Their big attractions are they are often easy to do; they make us feel like we have accomplished something because we can check it off our list; they are usually easy to do because we are good at doing them; they can create a false sense of momentum because we experience quick successes with them.

    However, they are not really worth the time we invest in them. For example, attending the monthly town hall meeting for two hours when you can get the minutes from the session the next day.

    These are activities that can usually be easily dropped off the "to-do" list and will create 10–20 percent more time and space for people to focus on what really matters. The key takeaway here is that unless you can lessen the workload, new stuff will not get done. This will take some discipline and time on the part of every supervisor but will greatly enhance the changes of the new strategic plan actually getting implemented.

TEAM PROTOCOL 2:
Learn How to Conduct an After Action Review (AAR)[31]

After Action Reviews (AARs) are a learning method developed by the US Army in the 1970s to help soldiers learn from both their mistakes *and* achievements. As I have mentioned before, both success and failure leaves clues, and an effective AAR can produce a powerful database for teams and work groups to review and apply the lessons learned to future efforts. It is a structured review process that uses four basic focus questions to organize the discussion:

AAR Review Questions (some variation of these four questions)

1. What did we set out to do? (What was our intention?)

2. What actually happened? (What did we do?)

3. What caused our results? (Why did it happen?)

4. What will we sustain/improve? (What can we do better next time?)

Don't be fooled by the simplicity of these focus questions. When conducted effectively, they will reveal a wealth of information. It is usually very helpful to have an identified, *quality facilitator* help the group move through the process and make sure everyone participates, especially the leader. AARs are *not* gripe sessions or intended to blame or embarrass anyone. They are a *learning process* that can make groups and teams smarter and better prepare them for future events and issues.

They are also *risky* endeavors because they assume that the organizational culture supports honesty, openness, feedback, and transparency. If that does not describe your campus culture, don't attempt an AAR because it could turn into a deeply critical and harmful review.

Years ago, I witnessed an AAR debrief about a campus "incident" (a student was severely injured on the campus) and the poor response

---

31 Darling, M., Parry, C. & Moore, J. (2005). Learning in the Thick of It. *Harvard Business Review.* https://hbr.org/2005/07/learning-in-the-thick-of-it.

to it. Leaders didn't know what was going on, communicated poorly with each other, and got in each other's way. The HR Vice President didn't know how to actually conduct an AAR; although he knew the theory, it got real ugly fast, with finger pointing and blaming. Instead of following the prescribed process, participants began to complain about each other's leadership, highlighting how others dropped the ball in responding to the incident and declaring that they should have been in charge of the response and communication process. You want to avoid this at all costs because it will strike fear throughout the team or group and people will never forget the experience.

If you are going to build your capacity for conducting an AAR, I suggest you begin with successes first and then, if appropriate, migrate to mistakes and missteps. *If* the right conditions exist, it can be one of the most effective ways to learn as a group, but it does have risk attached to it.

Sometimes AARs are called postmortems, which are conducted after a project is completed. But if you are involved in a long-term change process or initiative, you can use AARs periodically to stop the momentum of an initiative, reflect on what has happened, and learn from it as you move forward. This protocol can build learning into the entire process. It will take discipline to do this but will be well worth the effort.

Implementation Note:

There is an excellent article from the *MIT Sloan Management Review* titled "Learn When to Stop Momentum,"[32] which shows you how to take periodic timeouts during an implementation process or change initiative and identify what's working and what's not and, most importantly, learn as you go.

AARs are used extensively throughout the armed forces and in many corporations. They are only now seeing some use on campuses but

---

32 Barton, M. A. & Sutcliffe, K. M. (2010). Learn When to Stop Momentum. *MIT Sloan Management Review*. https://sloanreview.mit.edu/article/learning-when-to-stop-momentum/.

they can help a campus become smarter and build its resilience *if* they apply what they are learning to future implementation efforts.

Implementation Note:

There is an excellent video titled "Conducting Effective After Action Reviews (AAR) Part 1."[33] It depicts a group of fire rangers debriefing an exercise, and they walk through the process carefully and thoughtfully.

AARs can be conducted in person (my preference) or electronically, where participants answer the focus questions and solicit input from other group or team members. Individual comments are *not* shared outside the group but "lessons learned" from the debrief can be circulated to appropriate parties throughout the campus.

The following are lessons learned from a recent strategic planning process that didn't go very well. It became bogged down with too much "process" because it tried to include too many people and people became overwhelmed with too much information to meaningfully absorb. I was asked to conduct an AAR about the process so that the president's cabinet could learn from it.

The guiding principles stated by the president were:

> We need to extract as much learning as we can from this recent planning process. I realize that people worked very hard and took this seriously. We are not looking to blame anyone, and I don't want any names attached to the results. Please help us be smarter in the future. I am very appreciative of your efforts with this project.

The president's framing of the review created a constructive context for the AAR because now the group was in "service" of the institution. Overall, the climate of the debrief group was very positive and people felt safe enough to be honest about what happened. These

---

33 PublicResourceOrg. (2010). Conducting Effective After Action Reviews (AAR) Part
    1. YouTube video. https://www.youtube.com/watch?v=74Afb8qLujo.

lessons were captured, vetted by the president's cabinet, and sent electronically to all leaders on the campus.

Some lessons that were produced from the review

1. Senior leadership's meaningful involvement is critical to success (e.g., attend planning meetings, read the reports and respond, talk about the importance of the planning process). This was lacking with our recent planning efforts.

2. A transparent and robust communication process is important. People need to trust the communication process if they are going to believe the planning process is credible (e.g., tell the truth during the data gathering process, both our strengths and weaknesses). It is important to have a combination of high tech (newsletters and updates) and high touch (town hall meetings, small group discussion, planning updates *throughout* the planning process). We relied too much on technology and not enough on face-to-face communication.

3. Make sure you have *meaningful* engagement of campus stakeholders, *especially faculty*. If faculty aren't really involved in creating the plan, you will not get it implemented. Be committed to listen to everyone—capture their ideas and put them into a shared database so that others can review them. This kind of transparency can build trust in the process.

4. Make sure you don't fall into the trap of "listening to yourselves too much." Be disciplined about seeking an external perspective (e.g., look at national issues and trends in higher education, seek the perspectives of external stakeholders). We did a good job of soliciting ideas and perspectives from internal stakeholders but could have engaged more external people and organizations.

5. Realize that trust is a "strategic asset." You need to pay attention to building "relational capital" throughout the planning implementation process. You can do this by being transparent with all the data that is gathered throughout the process, defining the "decision rules" (who is going to do what), telling the truth, especially about difficult news, and listening to multiple perspectives).

You get the idea…short, sweet, and powerful lessons any leader on the campus can utilize in their change or planning efforts in the future. No names are ever attached to the comments or lessons. You do not need a long and lengthy academic white paper that obscures what happened and muddles thing up. Clear and succinct is the way to go.

The above AAR took about one and a half hours and helped make the campus leaders smarter going forward. It was the first time a process was conducted like this *and* the results actually shared across the campus. Many people were pleased about the results and asked the HR function to provide AAR training for their individual units and departments.

If you can conduct multiple AARs on your campus about successes and failures, you will build your resiliency muscles because you will prize feedback and learning, open up communication channels throughout the institution, and make people smarter across the campus silos. All-powerful capacities to have when a crisis hits or a tough challenge rears its ugly head.

Here's the question you might ask yourself: "Could we do this process in my group/work unit/department /division school?"

TEAM PROTOCOL 3:
The Team Alignment Meeting

I have found the following set of questions helps a team, work group, or task force get on the same page regarding alignment. If you don't achieve alignment, implementation will be sporadic. These questions will take real thinking so you might want to take them in "chewable chunks" and answer a couple at a time, rather than tackle them all at once.

Team members should have this set of questions before the discussion takes place and think about them ahead of time so they are prepared to contribute to the conversation.

Lastly, these questions assume that there is a fair amount of openness and candor within the group. If there is mistrust present, unresolved conflict between group members, or a reluctance to have an honest conversation, these questions will not be helpful. This is a judgment call on the leader's part, so decide carefully.

1. **What are we trying to accomplish with this objective or goal?**

   Be specific with this question. You want to hear from everyone about how they see the team's goals and what exactly they are trying to accomplish. Capture their conversations on a flip chart or whiteboard for everyone to see.

   It is essential that every manager, director, or leader have a group conversation and discussion about alignment around their goals. This will take some time and attention but is well worth the investment. Do *not* assume that because you explain your team's goals and objectives, people will "get it." You need to create regular opportunities for discussion and dialogue about what you are trying to accomplish and where you are going with your implementation efforts.

2. **Why is this goal or objective important to us?**

   How does this make a real difference in the implementation of the strategic plan? In our professional lives? What do we get out of accomplishing this goal or objective (e.g., learn something new, need each other to accomplish this goal, stretch ourselves, add real value that is recognized by others)?

3. **How does it help the unit, division, or campus improve?**

   Be specific with this focus question because people need to see the connection between what they do and how it helps move the campus forward. The *why* is essential to implementation. Take the time to unpack this question and make the connection between what people are trying to accomplish and *how* it makes a difference.

4. **How will we accomplish this goal/objective?**

   This is where the real implementation discussion begins. Group members need to identify the steps and actions they need to commit to in order to accomplish the task. This might take some gentle prodding from the group leader but here is where you are creating an agreed upon "road map" for the team to follow.

   This does not mean that once you create the steps and actions you blindly follow the road map because things will inevitably change. It is important to get everyone on the same page as you to begin the journey. Periodic (monthly) check-ins are recommended to identify progress and challenges going forward.

5. **What are our measures of success?**

   How do we keep score as a team? (Remember to use lag and, most importantly, lead measures). How will we know that we have been successful?

   You want to make sure there is a level of specificity here. Creating a team "scorecard" is an important thing to do with implementation efforts. Make it as clear, understandable, and *simple* so you can and review it weekly.

6. **What might get in the way of us accomplishing our goal/objective?**

   Refer to the premortem design in the book to identify some of the anticipated challenges and hurdles. Make sure there is some agreement on potential challenges and encourage a discussion on *how* to deal with them going forward.

   This is an essential point: People have to think through and discuss the "how" so that they can own it. Everything looks good on paper but it's the clear steps forward that need to be understood by everyone on the team/group as they meet the integration challenges they will face together.

7. **What are we currently doing that is aligned with the new goal/objective?** There are usually tasks and activities taking place

currently that can be continued to help accomplish the planning goals and objectives. (If you have a completely new goal, then this focus question might not be appropriate.)

Digging Deeper—an option to consider

The next set of questions should be answered *anonymously* due to their sensitivity. This can be a simple procedure where you create a one-page survey of these suggested questions and distribute it to the team members. Make sure you protect the anonymity of team members' responses to ensure you get honest and accurate information. This can be done by using a trusted third party to organize the information and create a brief report for review (e.g., HR, an external consultant, a dean from another school).

If you believe your team members can have an open and honest exchange about these questions and the trust level is high, then by all means, have an open discussion about them. But here's the thing, in the "collegial" and conflict avoidance culture of higher ed, people will often soft sell any "problems" or challenges. This hurts implementation efforts deeply. You want to avoid this at all costs. I would strongly suggest that you conduct this short survey *anonymously*.

1. Do we have the *requisite talent* to accomplish this goal/objective? Please explain your answer.

2. Are our goals *realistic* and achievable in your opinion? Why? Why not?

3. Do you understand how *you* meaningfully contribute to this goal?

4. Do you see the *connection* between what you do and what we need to accomplish?

5. Do we have the *resources* (e.g. technology, space, money) needed to accomplish this goal? If not, what additional resources are necessary?

6. What *concerns* do you have about accomplishing the stated goals for the team/group?

7. What is the best way for team members to communicate with each other? How often? What is the preferred medium (face-to-face, teleconference, web conference, texting, Zoom)?

As you can see, these questions are qualitatively different than the first set of alignment questions. These kinds of conversations rarely happen in my experience unless the team leader proactively creates the opportunity for them to be asked and answered.

Once you collate all the responses and a third party (e.g. Human Resources, another leader from a school or department) creates an informal report summarizing the responses, the team leader should conduct a conversation about the implications of the answers that were provided. This will take some courage and skill to conduct because you might find out that people have real concerns about the stated goals *or* do not believe the team has the requisite talent to successfully accomplish the goal *or* people believe the goal is not realistic and that they will fail.

There are no simple answers if you find out that there are some negative perceptions to the feasibility of your department's or division's goals. But as they say in the implementation business, "The good news is that you now know what the bad news is." This is not meant to be a trivial remark—it is an essential element of successful implementation efforts.

Most leaders don't have a clue about how their people feel or what they think about implementation efforts. With these discussion questions and the additional survey questions, you will have access to information leaders rarely have.

Armed with this kind of strategic information, you can problem solve together how to move forward. There are many protocols and practices you can use in this book to help get the team moving in the right direction.

TEAM PROTOCOL 4:
The Supervisory Dialogue[34]

My colleague, Dr. Rodney Napier, who introduced me to the concept many years ago, has influenced the following description of the "Supervisory Dialogue," which is a performance management process that creates the opportunity for supervisors to have a meaningful and effective conversation about shared expectations and goals

The term supervision might seem outdated to some people—terms like performance appraisal and performance review are more frequently used, but I like the term supervision because it describes the *ongoing relationship*, not just the evaluation between the group/team leader and their direct reports.

In the following pages, you will learn about a highly effective supervision process that has been used in a variety of organizations (e.g., a nuclear power plant, several university campuses, many government agencies at the state and city level, school districts, a large insurance company, and a hedge fund) very successfully. By "successful" I mean the consistent application of this process produced powerful organizational and team results. Hundreds of participants have reported that it has helped them take their teams to a new level of play, helped change their organizational culture toward a positive and effective one, and vastly improved the relationships between supervisors and their direct reports.

To conduct the Supervisory Dialogue correctly takes time and attention. Anything of real value needs to be thoughtfully applied over time. People who have experienced it—even those who initially were reluctant or skeptical—report that the time invested is well worth the outcomes produced.

The research on supervision[35] indicates that most organizations spend somewhere between one and two hours on employee supervision a year. Often, these tend to be perfunctory sessions, utilizing

---

34 Sanaghan, P. & Eberbach, K. *Creating the Exceptional Team.*
35 Ibid.

checklists and focusing on a one-way dialogue from the supervisor to the employee. Many are dreaded moments where employees feel judged and evaluated with little understanding of their boss' expectations. Others are demotivating because the standards seem ridiculously high and a 2.7 on a 5-point scale doesn't make much sense and it sure doesn't feel very good.

What could be an opportunity for a great discussion, sharing of ideas and perspectives, and creating a plan for development moving forward is instead a tedious, morale-wasting experience. There has to be a better way.

Ideally, the timeframe for the Supervisory Dialogue is one year. In an ongoing team (e.g., student affairs, marketing, development, communications, IT) or a team that is working on a long-term project (e.g., implementing a campus-wide technology system, a branding/image campaign, a change management task force), the Supervisory Dialogue is a powerful mechanism for achieving excellence.

The Guiding Principles of the Supervisory Dialogue

The primary focus of the Supervisory Dialogue is the success of the team/group member.

The Supervisory Dialogue assumes that most employees are intelligent, hardworking and well-intentioned. The Supervisory Dialogue builds on the strengths of the team/group member, *not* their weaknesses. Although it acknowledges all team/group members have areas of needed development, it concentrates on the many gifts people bring to the table. It also articulates the support the leader and the organization is willing to provide the members to ensure their success.

A reality check: We realize there are difficult or problem employees. This represents about 5 percent of the total workforce and they can be very hard to deal with effectively. The Supervisory Dialogue is for the 95 percent of the workforce who are not "difficult" or "problem" employees. There are other processes, like Progressive Discipline, that can be utilized with those challenging individuals.

Supervision must be valued by the organization

This means that managers and leaders who are supervising people need to be trained, supported, and *rewarded* for effective supervision. In my experience, this is rarely the case on most campuses. Effective supervision communicates to everyone throughout the organization that investing time, attention, and support in people is an institutional *value*. It also communicates that honest feedback, rigorous goal setting, good communication, and developing people is *prized* by the organization.

It is all about building an honest and authentic relationship between leaders and their direct reports

Without authentic and meaningful relationships, real supervision can never take place. The leader and direct reports need to feel connected to each other, feel respected by each other, and believe that both parties in the Supervisory Dialogue are well-intentioned. This positive relationship enables both parties to explore possibilities together, be open to each other's ideas, negotiate differences effectively, and improve overall performance. This leads us to the next key principle.

Trust is essential

The Supervisory Dialogue will only serve both parties effectively if there is a fair amount of trust in the relationship between the leader and their direct report. Without some real trust, the dialogue will be guarded, the team/group members will endeavor to negotiate minimal goals and take little risk. As trust is created, the members will share more, take on bigger responsibilities, and stretch themselves to achieve more meaningful goals. The Supervisory Dialogue can create real trust between the leader and their direct reports because it creates an authentic discussion between two people. There is mutual accountability, support, and some shared openness.

The team member is in a vulnerable position in the Supervisory Dialogue process

The leader is in the "power" position because they can either reward or punish their direct reports. This human dynamic is rarely discussed about supervision but it is present in every supervisor/supervisee relationship. This is not a bad thing but needs to be acknowl-edged and the leader needs to be conscious about this ever-present dynamic.

The team leader needs to be proactive in establishing a safe and trust-ing relationship with their direct reports. They can do this by listen-ing carefully, providing clear examples of performance, focusing on the strengths of the individual, giving honest feedback, and being interested in the development of the employee.

People know when their boss values them as a person—it can't be faked. If respect is present in the relationship, the power dynamic is lessened, but it is always present. The leader needs to be conscious and considerate about this.

Guiding Questions for the Supervisory Dialogue

1. When you look back over the past year, what stands out to you regarding what you have accomplished? Please be specific.

2. What have been some important "lessons learned" from the past year?

3. What have been some challenges or difficulties you have encoun-tered over the last year or the last six months?

4. What are one or two areas of "needed development" you need to work on this year? How will you enhance your effectiveness?

5. What are some things you would like to accomplish over the next six to 12 months? Please provide a rationale for each goal and a simple way to measure them.

6. What education/training do you think you will need to be suc-cessful this upcoming year? Please be specific.

7. How can I be supportive as your supervisor?

Why these are effective Supervisory Questions.

An important note: I will walk you through the Supervisory Di-alogue carefully over the next few pages. The main thing to think about as you read about the process is that both parties would answer these focus questions *prior* to the supervisory meeting. You want to make sure that both parties have thoughtfully prepared for the meeting. This is "the" essential element to the process. Prior preparation as you will see shortly is vital to the success of the entire process.

1. **When you look back over the past year, what stands out to you regarding what you have accomplished? Please be specific.**

   The first question focuses on the positive accomplishments and successes of the team member. It creates the foundation for the *Supervisory Dialogue* and is the most important question in the entire process. The team member helps create a constructive context for the discussion by focusing initially on their contributions. It builds a positive base for the discussion to follow.

2. **What have been some important "lessons learned" from the past year?**

   This question assumes that the employee has actually learned some important things over the past year. This question asks the direct report to reflect upon what they have learned and deepens the conversation.

   These "lessons" can either be positive or negative. The direct report chooses the direction here and the leader should make sure not all the lessons are on the negative side. For example:

   a. "I learned that I am a little too ambitious about what I can realistically accomplish—I need to get reality checks before I commit to something."

   b. "I am a much better project manager than I originally thought. My group got all our major projects done on time this quarter."

   c. "I really have to work on my conflict resolution skills. I have avoided some important conversations that needed resolution."

    d. "My team is full of hardworking, dedicated people. I feel blessed to be their leader."

    e. "My people want to see me more often. I get caught managing the technical side of things and don't walk around and talk with folks."

    f. "We need to do a better job at boundary management with other teams and work groups throughout the division. As this initiative picks up more steam, we will be interacting with a lot of others."

3. **What have been some challenges or difficulties you have encountered over the past year?**

This question assumes there have been some "difficulties" and that it is helpful to identify them. This is not meant to be critical of the direct report or put them on the defensive. It is meant to begin to discuss some of the sensitive issues that need to be addressed. The Supervisory Dialogue is a holistic approach to supervision and deals with the good as well as the not so great. Both are needed if the supervisory process is going to have real integrity.

By posing the question, the direct report has the choice and freedom to acknowledge that everything hasn't been "perfect." It is important that the direct report not dodge it by saying something vague like, "There were a couple of glitches last year but nothing worth talking about." They are soft selling their challenges. The leader should be ready with their prepared examples to provide more rigor to the discussion. (This question will be a diagnostic about how open and honest the direct report really is about their shortcomings.)

4. **What are one or two areas of "needed development" you need to work on this year? How will you enhance your effectiveness?**

This question begins to move into a sensitive area because the direct report must be willing to admit they do have some things that need improvement. If there isn't a level of trust and a positive relationship present, the direct report will be reluctant to share this.

This is another reason the leader prepares their answers to the questions before the meeting. If the team member has some difficulty with this, the leader can then suggest some ideas and continue the dialogue.

I have found that most employees are all too willing to talk about their weaknesses and downplay their many strengths. This is why you only ask for one or two areas of needed development, not seven or eight. If most people focus on improving one, possibly two areas, they will have done well. The supervisor needs to make sure that their direct reports own their contributions as well as their areas of needed development.

What is important to pay attention to is *how* improving their areas of "needed development" will enhance their effectiveness as a team/group member. They must be clear about this because they need to believe it is well worth the time and effort to improve. They must understand the tangible benefits for improving.

For example: "By learning the Critical Path Planning software program, I will improve my overall project management skills and keep my unit's work on track" or "By improving my decision-making skills, I will be better prepared for the upcoming project we will undertake next month."

5. **What are some things you would like to accomplish over the next six to 12 months? Please provide a brief rationale for each goal and a simple way to measure them.** It is important that the direct report share what they believe they need to accomplish in order to contribute meaningfully to the team's/group's goals. The fact that both parties have thought carefully about this question beforehand creates a "reality check" for the direct report. If they go off on a tangent that really doesn't focus on the team's goals, the leader can provide some strong ideas about this.It is important to have a rationale that is well thought out because the leader can diagnose the effectiveness and strate-

gic nature of the member's thinking. The toughest element of this question is the *measurability* of the outcomes. Too often, individuals focus on activities (doing lots of things) and outputs rather than outcomes. For example:

- "I will accurately complete the monthly audit report on time." (There is no "fuzziness" about this.)

- "I will reduce the number of customer complaints in my unit by 30 percent in the first half of the year." (Note: They didn't go for a high number like 90 percent. The 30 percent figure seems doable.)

- "I will reduce the office expenses (e.g., photocopying, telephones, computers, electricity) by 15 percent by the end of the year."

- "I will work with Human Resources and provide training in decision-making for everyone in my unit. I will also work with HR to assess the effectiveness of my direct reports decision-making skills throughout the year."

- "I will spearhead Project X and successfully complete it on time and under budget."

6. **What education/training do you think you will need to be successful this upcoming year? Please be specific.** At this stage, you have a great deal of helpful information regarding the learning and development needs of the direct report. They will have discussed what they have learned, identified their areas of needed development, and their future goals. This information creates a *Learning Agenda* for the direct report.[36] This "agenda" should focus both on their strengths and areas of needed development for the employee. The leader needs to solicit the direct reports ideas about their educational and learning needs.

For example, if a team/group member realizes they need help managing their time, selected courses should be identified and participation ensured. Other examples might include visiting other departments on the campus to learn about best practic-

---

36 Sanaghan, P., Goldstein, L., & Jurow, S. (2001). A Learning Agenda for Chief Business Officers. NACUBO.

es, choosing a mentor to seek advice and wise counsel, receive coaching on a specific area of needed development, read an article or book about a specific topic to continue to build on a strength, attend a management or leadership program, write a paper on lessons learned about a particular project, or take an assertiveness course.

Everyone on the leader's team/group should have a "learning agenda" that they are working on throughout the next six to 12 months. Often, each direct report shares their learning agenda with their coworkers—this way everyone knows what others are working on. Having this information is helpful in several ways:

a. It communicates that everyone is focusing on improving, which becomes a team/group norm.It can create the opportunity for team/group members to help each other. If one team/group member is strong in an area where another member needs help, a natural support network can be created.

b. It creates a thoughtful risk-taking opportunity for everyone. Sharing your agenda lets everyone know that you know what you need to work on. This shared risk tends to build a stronger team/group feeling.[37]

7. **How can I be supportive as your supervisor (e.g., spend more time with you, provide access to outside resources, provide more timely feedback)?**

This question is important because it communicates to the direct report that the leader is committed to their success and they want to be supportive. It is essential that the leader probe a little with this question because members might be reluctant to ask for help.

The leader can suggest ways they can be helpful:

---

37 Sanaghan, P. & Eberbach, K. *Creating the Exceptional Team.*

a. How would you like us to communicate over the next six months? Face-to-face weekly meetings? A working lunch every month?

b. What should we agree to do if you encounter a problem or get stuck on a project? How can we be proactive when this happens?

c. Can you identify any company hurdles (e.g., politics, resources, connections) that might get in the way of successfully completing your goals? How can I be helpful with them?

d. The key here is for the leader to commit to *specific* support and follow through with them. This will build trust and credibility on the leader-member relationship.

Note: remember that both parties should come to the meeting with prepared answers to the seven focus questions.

The Initial Supervisory Meeting: This meeting would take place yearly and be approximately 1½–2 hours in duration. This meeting would be an in-depth discussion reviewing the team members' progress, accomplishments, and contribution in work of the previous year. The seven questions create the framework for this discussion.

Monthly "Check-Ins:" These are brief, *scheduled* meetings (30 minutes) to maintain the dialogue, right size expectations, provide feedback, and continue to build the leader/member relationship. A team/group member should *never* be surprised at the end of the year that they have not met their agreed upon goals or that their performance is less than stellar. These check-ins prevent this from happening. A short (one page) summary of this meeting should be captured in written format and given to both parties.

A "Half Time" Check-In: This meeting would be conducted approximately six months after the initial meeting and be formal in nature. It should take about one hour and have some structure to it. You can use the seven questions as a framework or create your own. The primary purpose of this *half-time* check in is to: Make sure everyone is on the same page, identify what has been accomplished to date and what needs to be completed, identify what has changed in the environment, and how this influences/impacts the team/group members' goals going forward and determine what is reasonable to accomplish over the next six months. You will have a good track record and database to reflect upon as you negotiate the future goals and accomplishments.

This proposed model takes some real and meaningful investment of time on the team leader's part, but in my experience it is the very best investment the leader can make to ensure stellar performance.

If you do the math, this process will take about 1–2 percent of a supervisor's time per employee in a given year. If you have six direct reports, that adds up to 10–12 percent of your management time. That's a great investment of your time.

TEAM PROTOCOL 5:
The Meeting Evaluation Survey

I have designed and delivered over 1,000 meetings over the past 30 years and written extensively about them.[38] [39] The bad and sad news about meetings is that way too many of them are ineffective.[40] [41]

In the group development field there is a theory called the "Rule of Four," which tells us that in a group of 10 to about 40 people, four people will do most of the talking. This lives large in higher education because of the faculty hierarchies that exist. Staff and administrators will often defer to faculty, and faculty can take over a conversation rather quickly.

If you want to build in an implementation mentality for your team, conducting highly effective meetings is one of the most powerful leverage points you can have.

---
38 Sanaghan, P. & Eberbach, K. *Creating the Exceptional Team.*
39 Sanaghan, P. and Gabriel, P. A. (2014). *Collaborative Leadership in Action.* HRD Press.
40 Lencioni, P. (2004). *Death by Meeting.* Jossey-Bass.;
41 Rogelberg, S. (2019). *The Surprising Science of Meetings.* Oxford University Press.

Meetings are at the very heart of a team's ongoing life. Effective teams and group teams conduct highly effective meetings consistently.[42] One of the most effective protocols they follow is the regular and *anonymous* assessment of the effectiveness of their team meetings.

The following five questions are all you need to obtain the information you need to continue to improve your meetings. You would hand these out at the end of a regular meeting and have participants fill them out before they leave to ensure a 100 percent return. No names are attached to this survey.

1. On a scale of 1–10 (1 being poor, 5 average, and 10 excellent) how would you rate today's team meeting?

2. How involved did you feel on a scale of 1–10? (You want to make sure that people feel involved psychologically and intellectually in all team meetings.)

3. What did you like most about the team meeting?

4. What did you like least? (No personal feedback, e.g., "Pat talks way too much;" rather, "Certain individuals seem to be dominating discussions.")

5. Any advice, suggestions, remarks? (This gives participants free reign to share what they liked about the meeting, ideas to improve future meetings, etc.)

It only takes a few minutes to answer the five focus questions and have people fill out the survey *anonymously* so that you get honest answers. It's also a helpful idea to have participants fill out the five questions *before* they leave the meeting or you will get a poor response rate.

Publish the anonymous remarks as part of the meeting minutes as soon as possible.

If you can commit to doing this kind of evaluation *over time*, listening to the results and incorporating the anonymous feedback, you will create outstanding meetings. This is such a simple process but

42 Sanaghan, P. & Eberbach, K. *Creating the Exceptional Team.*

do not be fooled by this. It's a "game changer" and one of the most powerful ideas I have seen over my 30-year career.

If you have the courage to periodically evaluate your meetings with this tool, you will be able to have great implementation results.

By evaluating your meetings, you communicate several things to everyone on the team:

1. That their ideas, feedback, and advice are valued and can make a difference.

2. That the team is committed to learning and ongoing feedback is an important process in the learning journey.

3. That you value their time and want to use it well.

TEAM PROTOCOL 6:
Defining the "Decision Rules"

At the end of the day, effective decision-making either makes or breaks an implementation process. When there is "fuzziness" about what people can and cannot do, the larger system gets frozen and things move at a glacial pace. If people cannot decide, they cannot act effectively. They will be frozen in place because they are unsure if it is okay to move forward, allocate resources, and take risks. It is the death of implementation and execution efforts.For decades, the notion of pushing decision-making down to the lowest appropriate level has been more of a platitude than a reality. Leaders tend to hold onto their decision-making authority and often quite vague about the "decision rules" for their people. We cannot afford this to be the situation when it comes to implementation. Leaders need to be dedicated to clarity and this decision protocol will clear up any confusion about *who makes what decisions.*

The following simple decision-making model has been around for many years and has been modified and enhanced over time. It works well with task forces, implementation teams, and work groups. It is a leadership decision-making model that *clarifies* how decisions will get made in the group. It has five levels that are identified by the group/team leader *before* decisions are made. This is essential to remember. The group/team needs to understand who is making what decision so they can act accordingly.

Level I: These decisions are made by the group leader with no input or advice from others. It is an autocratic decision and should be used judiciously.

Level II: This is when the leader seeks input, advice, and ideas from *individuals*. Often, this solicitation of ideas raises the expectation that the leader will actually listen to the advice and *do* exactly what people suggested. The leader needs to manage the expectations of the advice givers by stating, up front, that they have a decision to make and that they want to use the individual as a "thought partner" *but* the leader will make the final decision.

Level III: This is when the group leader openly discusses an issue or decision with many people sometimes over time, if it is a complex decision. Once again, the leader clarifies *up front* (e.g., "I have an important decision to make and I want lots of idea sharing and feedback *but* in the end, I will make the final decision"). The leader has to proactively manage the expectations of others in the group.

Level IV: This is when the group leader is willing to *trust* the group to make an effective decision and acts as a *"peer of the realm"* with one "vote," just like everyone else in the group.

They have to have a fair level of confidence in the competence and character of the group members before they use this level of decision-making. But this is where high performing teams live.[43]

They also cannot change their minds in the middle of the decision-making process if they don't like where things are headed.

Level V: This is a "delegated" decision where the leader shares the intended outcomes of a decision with others (e.g., decide who needs to be on the curriculum revision committee), agrees on a commu-

---

43 Ibid.

nication protocol that keeps them informed of progress (not micro-managing), and lets the group make the final decision.

When people know what level of decision-making they are dealing with, they understand their authority boundaries and can move effectively within them. Implementation is vastly improved because clarity allows people to move forward with actions.

You can determine the level of implementation effectiveness by looking at how a group or task force moves between the decision levels. If they are frozen between levels I and II, very little will be accomplished. When implementation is flourishing, levels IV and V are used often.

CHAPTER 5

The Tool Box

Team Tool 1: Self-Managed Groups

Self-managed groups will leverage the time and productivity of large groups.

Use them when:

- Several groups are working simultaneously on a task or a large number of participants in a meeting divide into smaller groups for a meaningful discussion.
- You want to provide a structure for groups to accomplish a certain task and be fully responsible for the outcome of their work.

The Activity:

1. Tell participants that each group they form will be self-managing, in other words, responsible for its own work product and process. Note that you won't be checking on them, although you will be available to clarify the task, if needed.

2. Let all participants know that they need to identify people within their small work groups to take responsibility for one of the roles. This should be done *before* the group starts work. This is a key element because people tend to dive into the task quickly

and the "more assertive" people can quickly dominate the discussion.

3. Distribute a handout summarizing the various roles or show them on a large screen. You may want to review the various roles and their respective responsibilities using the following notes for guidance:

The **Recorder** captures the group's work on the flip chart. The facilitator may want to suggest that people assigned to record the group's work don't become trapped in traditional roles. If, for example, the work group includes an administrative assistant they should not automatically be assigned the role of recorder.

The **Presenter** shares the small group's work with all the participants in the meeting. Many people will want this high-profile role but top leaders should avoid it. Suggest that other people volunteer to serve as the group's presenter.

The **Timekeeper** gently reminds the group of how much time it has to accomplish the task. For example, if given an hour to discuss a problem and create some solutions, the timekeeper would remind group members about every 10 or 15 minutes how much time remains. (This is a great role for top leaders, provided they only remind people and don't aggravate them by creating stress. ("Let's get going here!" "We're running out of time!")

The **Facilitator** makes sure that all the participants are engaged and involved and that everything remains on track so the group can accomplish the end task. This can involve managing a dominant personality who may start taking over the group. Because verbal people often volunteer for this role, you might want to deliver this message: "The role of facilitator is challenging. The main purpose is to ensure that everyone in the group participates. If you are doing a lot of talking, you are not facilitating!"

As participants move into their smaller work groups, remind them to assign the roles right after the entire group has congregated and *before* any work begins.

This simple technique will help large groups become an effective work group. People will almost always take their roles seriously and help the group accomplish its task. Please use it.

TEAM TOOL 2:
The Responsible, Accountable, Consulted, and Informed Parties (RACI) Chart

This tool is primarily a decision-making process that helps clarify roles, responsibilities, and authority among stakeholders involved in either making decisions or taking action. When it is fuzzy about "who does what," implementation efforts falter.

It helps create a discussion about people's level of involvement regarding decisions and actions and is especially useful with cross-boundary efforts between divisions and departments.

When there is role confusion within a department or between two departments, conflict can occur. This tool can help create clarity about the *most important* decisions and actions and should *not* be used for everything or you will bog down in process.

The RACI Chart has several benefits

1. It can clarify overlapping, redundant, or inconsistent responsibilities.

2. It can structure a discussion that enables participants to distribute authority and establish clear lines of communication.

3. It can resolve any functional issues that commonly arise between departments.

4. It helps to clearly define the roles and responsibilities of team members who are working on a project.

5. It helps to eliminate role confusion.

6. It can identify when to provide input.

7. It helps define the scope of individuals' responsibilities and clarifies expectations.

The Four Key Roles

1. **Responsible** ("the doer"): This is the person who performs a task or body of work. They are responsible for the task. Others can be assigned to *assist* in the work required but one person is ultimately responsible for completing the task. No veto power.

2. **Accountable** ("the buck stops here"): The individual or role holding ultimate responsibility and the ability to say yes or no. They must sign off on the decision/action. They are the "approver" for the work the responsible person provides. There should be only one "accountable" party.

3. **Consulted** ("in the loop"): The individual or role who provides feedback, advice, opinion. They have input but no real influence over how things will move forward (e.g., subject matter experts) *before* the decision/action is taken. No veto power.

4. **Informed** ("in the picture"): The individual or role that is informed *after* the decisions are made. No input.

Clear Points

To do this right takes real time and attention. I can't emphasize this enough. It looks simple on paper but can be a challenge to implement. Do not undertake this process if you are not willing to take the time to resolve the conflicts that will surface.

The RACI Chart clarifies things and it will surface some issues and tensions. For example, I might think that I need to be consulted before the decision to implement something goes forward. The team leader might think that I only need to be informed after the fact. This could surface confusion about my role and contribution within the team.

- Use the RACI Chart to identify important functions and processes. It is *not* useful for everything.

- If you have more than one "R" (responsible), which can happen, make sure you identify a *lead* "R" so, if something happens, you know who to hold accountable.

- Watch out for more than one "A." This should be a rare occurrence because it can reduce ultimate accountability because each party might assume the other is paying attention to the implementation process.

- You might start with a generic example first when using the RACI Chart. Have people think through several non-threatening examples before they deal with real issues. Make sure people know how to use the process before delving into real decisions and tasks.

- If you have two groups working together trying to define "who does what," it is helpful to have each individual fill out the entire RACI Chart *anonymously*, then plot all the answers on a flip chart/white board/PowerPoint for everyone to see. Notice the common ground ideas, if you have some, then tackle the areas where there are unclear expectations.

- This will take some time and discussion but stick with it because this will build clarity and discipline between the two groups and help with the collaborative implementation efforts.

- You should evaluate how effective the RACI Chart is working after one week to be proactive about its operational value. It doesn't take long to determine if it's effective or not. Periodic reviews will be necessary, simply because thing can change quickly so pay attention to it. This is not a one and done tool.

TEAM TOOL 3:
Creating S.M.A.R.T. Goals and Objectives

This planning tool or device has been around for many years and was made famous by Peter Drucker, the late, great management thinker, who also introduced the Management by Objectives (MBO) approach over half a century ago. It tends to feel very comfortable to linear thinkers, who value specificity and details. It won't work for everybody but with implementation efforts you need all the tools you can get.

This can become a tedious and complicated process if you aren't careful with it. Its greatest contribution is that it helps make people really think about what they are trying to accomplish. People often need to practice a little with it before they become comfortable using this tool. Having a thought partner walk through the steps and thinking with you is always a helpful process.

I have adapted this tool a little to make it more user friendly:

- **Specific:** What exactly will you accomplish? (This should be stated in clear and unambiguous terms. Keep it short—a lot of words won't help.)

- **Measurable:** How will you know when you have reached this goal or objective? (What will success look like?)

- **Achievable:** Is achieving this goal/objective realistic? (This is an essential question. Does the person(s) have the requisite talent, experience, and resources to achieve this goal/objective? This is where a thought partner or good supervision comes in handy.)

- **Relevant:** Why is the goal/objective meaningful/significant to you? (What benefit will you get from accomplishing this goal/objective (e.g., learn something new, contribute to the team)? Is it aligned with where we need to go?)

- **Timely:** When will you achieve this goal or objective. (Is there a realistic time frame? Are there "mini" deadlines that can keep you on track?)

Once again, this tool and way of thinking might take some practice, but it can be a useful device when organizing implementation efforts.

TEAM TOOL 4:
"Post-it" Feedback

During a collaborative planning and implementation process there will be many opportunities to present ideas and solicit feedback. Many of the meeting designs/practices and protocols in this book actively solicit feedback from stakeholders. Feedback creates the opportunity to enhance ideas and provides a reality check on the practicality of suggestions and ideas.

Unfortunately, there is a downside to feedback that needs to be managed by the collaborative implementation leader. We have witnessed planning groups, task forces, and steering committees making presentations to others on their campuses and see the feedback process become a critical and demoralizing process. What should have been an opportunity to build and strengthen ideas becomes a "turkey shoot" where the critics prevail and ideas—and sometimes even people—are personally battered. Once you have experienced a meeting like this, enthusiasm for future presentations quickly fades.

Negative feedback rarely improves the quality of ideas but continues to persist on many campuses. The challenge for the implementation leader is to create a constructive feedback process where criticism has its place but does not become the overriding factor in a discussion of ideas. The goal is to obtain effective and honest feedback and create both emotional and intellectual safety in the process.

The beauty of this simple technique is that it gets everyone's ideas in the room, *especially* the less verbal participants. It also neutralizes the power of the critics while still getting their ideas in the room.

In this activity, we are going to assume that five to eight participants have been working in small groups on developing an action plan and are ready to present their beginning ideas to others in the larger group of 40.

The Activity: when participants are ready to make their presentations, the facilitator/leader informs everyone before the presentations are made that the feedback process is going to be a little different.

Make sure that all participants have some large (3 x 5) Post-its, about 10–12 per participant. Inform everyone that they should use the Post-its to write down their feedback regarding the action plan presentations. Their written feedback can address any of the following three elements:

1. **What participants like about the ideas presented by others.** It is always nice to hear what people appreciate about ideas so encourage this (e.g., this action plan addresses an important challenge we have been avoiding, I really like the way you are involving students with the "One Stop" shopping project).

2. **Suggestions to improve the ideas presented.** Examples include: "Your communication plan seems very one way. You need to build in more interaction where campus stakeholders have the opportunity to provide feedback and ideas," "The action plan feels rather vague to me—can you be more specific? Provide more details?"

3. **Resources to share.** This could include people's names, suggested contacts, books, research that would help leverage or enhance the effectiveness of the suggested action plans presented. Examples include:

   a. "You should contact Jim Seitz in Marketing, he is an expert on this topic."

   b. "I can put you in touch with some of the faculty members at Incredible University who have established a Center for Teaching Excellence."

With these kinds of offers, make sure the person writes their name on the Post-it!

It is always helpful to provide examples so that the participants clearly understand what kind of feedback you seek.

Facilitator/Leader Tip

In a group with low trust, or one that is very new at collaborative practices, this is an excellent way to solicit feedback in a nonthreatening way. As stakeholders get used to being more open, you can try a more direct approach where you solicit verbal feedback from participants. But err on the safe side whenever you can.

Let participants know that *after* each presentation, several minutes will be provided so that they can write down their feedback *anonymously* on Post-its. After they have written their feedback, have them place the Post-its on the appropriate flip chart. Then have the next presentation (this should take no more than two to four minutes per presentation).

Continue the process of: presentation, time for written feedback, and placing Post-its until all the presentations are completed and feedback provided.

The final step is to have each presenting group meet for 20 minutes to read the feedback on the sticky notes, react to the feedback, and reach a beginning agreement on how to include the suggestions for improvement and resource ideas where appropriate.

If possible, have each group make a brief (two-minute) presentation to the larger group to show how the feedback and suggestions helped or influenced their thinking. For example:

- "Most of the feedback was very positive."
- "We forgot to include the Staff Council in our planning process."
- "There is another campus that has already done this kind of implementation plan. We now have a contact to follow through with and learn how they did it."
- "People shared some different metrics for us to consider."

Three Informal Surveys

There are three *informal* surveys in this section:

1. An Implementation Survey

2. A Boundary Management Survey

3. A Culture Survey

These are *informal* assessments but are well informed by the research on implementation and my 30-year experience with strategic planning. They will not have the rigor of validated instruments but can give you a pretty good idea of what to pay attention to with these three very important organizational elements:

1. Understanding your capacity to actually implement important things is helpful to understand *before* you start the implementation process.

2. Learning what organizational boundaries you need to be aware of is vital to your success. They are out there and mostly invisible, that's what makes them so important to understand. For example, you can find that you are trying to move an initiative forward but if you have no real sponsor to help you through the difficult terrain, you will be a stranded asset quickly.

3. Getting a "picture" of your organizational culture is very important because, as Peter Drucker famously said, "Culture eats strategy for breakfast." Knowing the strengths and weaknesses of your campus culture is essential to the successful implementation of your plan.

For those individuals who prefer a more rigorous and "validated" approach, I suggest that you use the SPIES assessment.[44] I coauthored this instrument and I have used it effectively with about 30 campuses.

I also strongly suggest that anyone who takes these informal surveys should be *anonymous*, to ensure honest answers. If you have different stakeholder groups (e.g., faculty, staff, administrators) taking the survey, have the responders identify their specific stakeholder group only so that you can contrast and compare scores.

With all these surveys, summarize the answers and create an average for each statement. Then review the summary with those people who participated in the surveys. Even if the answers aren't very good (there is a good chance this will be the case), share them anyway because it's the respectful thing to do. Besides, they know what's really going on because they are living it and now they know you know what's going on!

The *Informal* Implementation Survey

The following questions have been informed by several researchers and academics in the fields of implementation and execution[45][46].

This informal survey can be used very effectively with specific groups (e.g., unit, division, departments, schools). It will provide a vivid picture of a group's perceptions about their capacity to implement their plans. Although this is an informal survey, it will give you an informative picture about how people on your campus experience their capacity to actually implement things. This is invaluable because understanding this *before* you begin to implement a strategic

---

44 Sanaghan, P. & Mrig, A. SPIES.
45 Bossidy, L., Charan, R., & Burck, C. Execution: *Getting Things Done.*
46 McChesney, C., Covey, S., & Huling, J. *The 4 Disciplines.*.

plan, a large-scale change process, or a strategic initiative, helps you pinpoint where you need to focus your efforts.

For example, if people report that collaboration is *not* rewarded, senior leadership can create a recognition and reward program to support implementation efforts. Or if you find that your supervisory process does *not* support implementation efforts, leadership can make sure that this is considered a priority for supervisors. It can act as a premortem[47] by revealing the strengths and weaknesses of your perceived capacity to implement things.

The Scoring Scale:

1 = Strongly disagree

2 = Disagree

3 = Neutral

4 = Agree

5 = Strongly agree

What Is the Campus Unit You Are Assessing?

- DepartmentDivisionWork unit SchoolCampusOther

  _____

A Baker's Dozen

1. The priorities of this (department, division, unit, and school) are clear and understood.

       1   2   3   4   5

2. Collaboration across our (department, division, unit, and school) is encouraged.

       1   2   3   4   5

---

47 Klein. Performing a Project Premortem.

3. People get recognized and rewarded for getting work accomplished.

      1   2   3   4   5

4. I believe we have enough resources (e.g., people, technology, space, and money) to accomplish our department's, division's, unit's, school's) goals and objectives.

      1   2   3   4   5

5. For the most part, people here (department, division, and unit) are good at getting things done.

      1   2   3   4   5

6. Our current supervisory/performance appraisal process supports the implementation of plans, initiatives, and change processes.

      1   2   3   4   5

7. We have effective communication processes that keep us informed about progress toward goals.

      1   2   3   4   5

8. I understand the "decision rules" with my implementation efforts (I know what I can and cannot do).

      1   2   3   4   5

9. I get enough support from my direct supervisor (e.g., time, attention, advice, feedback, problem solving, help with setting priorities) when it comes to my implementing the goals and objectives of this (department, division, unit, school).

      1   2   3   4   5

10. We know how "to keep score" regarding our goals and objectives. We know if we are making progress with our implementation efforts.

      1   2   3   4   5

11. It is okay to "fail intelligently" here (as long as the effort was invested and the intentions were good), less than successful efforts are not punished.

    1   2   3   4   5

12. We share "best practices" with each other on a regular basis.

    1   2   3   4   5

13. People are given enough support to succeed and are held accountable for lack of performance.

    1   2   3   4   5

Don't overthink this informal survey; it will either work for you or it won't. Keep asking yourself questions like:

1. What does "encouragement" mean?

2. What does "enough" resources actually mean?

3. What does "support" look like?

4. What does "effective communication" mean?

You get the idea—if you don't have any faith in the practical informality of this survey, then don't use it. Use something that is validated; then you will have confidence in the results.

A Little Story

Several years ago, I was helping facilitate a strategic planning process in a Research 1 institution in California. I always like to get a sense of the level of trust on a campus because this will tell me how hard or easy the planning process will be. I put together a five-question survey with some of the questions from the survey above and included one about campus trust.

The results weren't very good and I met with the Chancellor and senior staff. The Chancellor was a brilliant academic, whose discipline was dark matter. He was considered one of the foremost experts in the world on the subject. He didn't like the lack of rigor with the informal survey and was critical of the results.

I shared my thinking about the survey: We had 186 responses across the campus and it included six different stakeholder groups. The average score (and I know the academics won't like this) for trust was 2 on a scale of 5. I just wanted a snapshot about the level of trust and I think that this survey tells me that there might be an issue about trust on the campus.

He collegially dismissed the comment and the data and asked the Institutional Research Department (there were 12 of them) to survey the campus with a validated instrument.

When the results came back a couple of weeks later, the particular item about campus trust scored a 1.7. He conceded that there is a trust issue that needed to be paid attention to with the planning process going forward.

All this is to say, use what works for you. I coauthored a validated survey about implementation and execution—the SPIES—and it's a very good assessment, but I still think informal surveys can work pretty well. Your choice.

The *Informal* Boundary Management Survey

Unearthing The "Invisible" Barriers to Implementation

As a team or group begins to implement their action plans in service of the strategic plan, they need to pay special attention to what other groups are doing with their own implementation efforts. We all operate in a complex "system" of some kind and simply can't act in an isolated manner or we will bump into others along the way. Managing these *institutional boundaries*—whether they are interpersonal, political, informational, technological, or physical resources—are essential to team/group success.[48] [49] [50]

48 Hackman, J. R. ed. (1990). *Groups that Work (and Those That Don't)*. Jossey-Bass.;
49 Sanaghan, P., Goldstein, L., & Roy, A. (2004). *Change Management Readiness Survey*. HRD Press.
50 Sanaghan, P. & Eberbach, K. *Creating the Exceptional Team*.

This is especially important with implementation efforts because almost always, you will need the help of others in order to complete your tasks and activities. You can have the best implementation team or group in the world but if you don't understand the "political" network you must navigate, you will probably fail.

If you don't have a credible and trusted communication process that keeps people informed, throughout the campus, you can find yourself the victim of a robust "rumor mill."

Lastly, if you don't have agreed upon protocols and processes to deal with anticipated interdepartmental "problems" (e.g., conflict, loss of trust, poor resource allocation decisions,) you will be challenged to move things forward. These problems can kill implementation efforts quickly.

The following survey questions will provide an *informal* snapshot about your current boundary management strengths and weaknesses. You will need to pay attention to these "boundaries" throughout your implementation efforts.

The survey only deals with the campuses' *internal* boundary issues and *not* external stakeholder's boundary issues (such as vendors, community, business leaders). Once again, the answers to this survey should be *anonymous* to ensure honest responses. Distribute the survey to team/group members, collate the data, and create an informal report for discussion. Most importantly, create specific strategies to improve boundary management issues because they can stop implementation efforts cold.

I want to acknowledge the contribution of J. Richard Hackman from Harvard, who did most of his exceptional research on effective groups and teams. He was the first author I encountered that talked about the importance of "boundaries" and helped me understand how really good teams can fail if they don't understand all the organizational boundaries that are outside the team and how to manage them.

Even a great team will be a "stranded asset" if they don't handle the multiple boundaries well. I think that this is a "hidden" barrier for many teams, especially in higher education. The multiple cultures of higher education (e.g., faculty, staff, administration) are complex and difficult to manage at times. When you add in things like tradition, protocols, silos, hierarchy, faculty life, and a usually conflict adverse culture, these things rarely see the light of day.

This simple survey will raise your awareness about the multiple boundaries you need to pay attention to during the implementation phase.

Boundary Management Survey Questions

The Scoring Scale

1 = Strongly disagree

2 = Disagree

3 = Neutral

4 = Agree

5 = Strongly agree

1. Our vice president (or the senior leader we report to) understands and supports our work.

    1   2   3   4   5

2. Other groups within our department/division understand what we are trying to accomplish.

    1   2   3   4   5

3. We know where we need to go if we need help and support from others.

    1   2   3   4   5

4. We understand the complexity of organizational politics and have the "savvy" necessary to navigate the politics and get things done.

    1   2   3   4   5

5. We communicate effectively with others throughout our department/division.

       1   2   3   4   5

6. We have constructive relationships with groups external to our department/division with whom we need to work with in order to implement our action/implementation plans.

       1   2   3   4   5

7. We know where to go for information or content expertise that will help us with our implementation efforts.

       1   2   3   4   5

8. Generally, we understand what others in our department/division are working on regarding implementing the strategic plan.

       1   2   3   4   5

9. I understand our team's/group's level of authority and decision-making power. We know what we can and cannot do.

       1   2   3   4   5

10. We have processes in place to deal with interdepartmental problems and conflicts when they occur.

       1   2   3   4   5

The Organizational Culture Survey

This survey has a little more rigor than the previous ones. All the focus questions are taken from the SPIES assessment. There are six categories in the SPIES assessment: Alignment, Decision-Making, Organizational Discipline, Collaboration, Culture, and Engagement and Inclusion.

I have used this survey with about 30 campuses, and they have found it helpful in deeply understanding their current capacity to implement their plan. One caution: The lowest scored category of all six is for Culture. The averages of the other five categories is about a 3.4. The Culture category averages a 2.2.

I say this to communicate that you might not get very high scores in this category, just food for thought.

The Scale

1 = Strongly disagree

2 = Disagree

3 = Neither agree nor disagree

4 = Agree

5 = Strongly agree

The Survey Questions

1. Internal politics rarely get in the way of getting things done on our campus.

    1   2   3   4   5

2. The natural boundaries between divisions, departments, and schools do not interfere with getting things done.

    1   2   3   4   5

3. We have a fair amount of "tolerance for failure" on our campus (e.g., people are not afraid to make mistakes. When mistakes happen, we try and learn from them and distill lessons learned).

    1   2   3   4   5

4. We don't get caught up in endless "processes" (e.g., having too many meetings, delayed decision-making, trying to include everyone in everything, waiting until we have all the information).

    1   2   3   4   5

5. Our faculty governance process (e.g. faculty senate, council) is effective.

1   2   3   4   5

6. There is little competition between departments and divisions.

1   2   3   4   5

7. The relationship between our senior leadership team and the faculty is constructive.

1   2   3   4   5

8. We can talk about sensitive issues in our department/division.

1   2   3   4   5

9. We are able to "speak truth to power" to our senior leadership team (e.g., provide honest feedback).

1   2   3   4   5

10. Overall, the trust level on this campus is high.

1   2   3   4   5

Once again, take the *anonymous* scores and create an average for each statement and an overall average for the culture category. If you find that you get a lot of 3s, that's probably not a good sign, in my view. I am not a statistician to say the least but I have found that a 3 is a "silent no" because people are on the fence about the statement and aren't willing really to make a choice one way or another. There is a big difference between a 4 and a 2 so many people opt out of a real score and settle for an okay answer. Just my perspective.

The Push Agenda: A Mini Case Study

Note: *I first learned about the Push Agenda from Reverend Dennis H. Holtschneider, former president of DePaul University. He utilized this process on his campus in the final year of a very successful strategic planning process that I helped facilitate.*

I have used this "push" process several times over the past few years and the clients seem to find it very helpful.

Context

The president convenes a large group (35–40) of senior leaders throughout the institution for two days to review the progress of the strategic plan. This group consists of all the deans, vice presidents, senior staff, provost, some highly regarded faculty, as well as the presidents of student government and staff council president.

The tone and tenor of these meetings are collegial and designed to encourage maximum interaction and cross-boundary dialogue. The outcome of this important meeting is a renewed sense of ownership, accomplishment, and momentum. This year, the president introduced the notion of a "Push Agenda" to real focus and clarity about what needed to be accomplished over the next year.

The president defined the Push Agenda as "a subset of our strategic plan, designed to identify priorities for the final years of the plan's realization. The Push Agenda does not supplant the campus strategic plan. However, some goals are designated for increased emphasis in the final year of the plan in order to move them ahead in an intentional manner."

The Push Agenda has two primary motivations behind it: It is critical that changes in the environment are identified, discussed, and understood by senior leaders. The implications of these changes, as well as how they influence and impact the current plan, is an important senior-leadership discussion.

It is essential that senior leaders "finish well" toward the end of a planning process. It is easy to lose motivation and focus or become a little too self-congratulatory after experiencing success. Creating real focus on what is essential to continue with the plan communicates that the strategic plan is a meaningful and important process to all stakeholders.

The "Design" of the Push Agenda retreat followed the following steps:

1. To start the retreat, the whole group conducted an informal environmental scan of the university to inform their thinking about potential issues, events, and trends impacting the institution. The design used was the Future Timeline, which is in Chapter 2.

    The Future Timeline is a collaborative meeting design that looks at the horizon issues and trends that the campus might face in the future. It's an excellent way to "see" the future from diverse perspectives and gets everyone on the same page generally speaking. It helps create a powerful shared context for the rest of the retreat because people are thinking about the information they collectively created in the Future Timeline, as they look at their current goals.

2. Participants self-selected one of the five strategic goals they wanted to review with colleagues. No one was assigned a goal. This is an important element with collaborative planning work. When people are able to choose what they want to work on, I have

found that they tend to be very interested and motivated to do great work.

3. Each group then spent 45 minutes discussing potential areas of focus for the next two years and "generally agreed" (not consensus) on a small set of recommendations for their goal area. They utilized "self-managed" groups which is described in Chapter 5·

4. Each group then presented their beginning recommendations about what needed to be done in their specific goal area and received constructive feedback from the entire group. We used the Post-it feedback tool described in Chapter 5. This anonymous feedback was captured for review later in the retreat.

Next Steps

In the early evening, the president convened a small, diverse group of eight leaders that were selected by participants to review the anonymous feedback that was received for each goal area. They created a second draft set of recommendations for review the next morning by the entire group. This took almost three hours and this smaller group worked very hard that evening in service of the larger group.

All the Post-it feedback was captured electronically and shared with the group the next morning to ensure transparency and accountability. Participants could review these notes as they wished.

The second draft was reviewed in a transparent way by the entire leadership group the next morning. Once again, participants self-selected the goal they wanted to work on for a *final* draft of the recommendations. This took about 30 minutes.

Then each group made a brief presentation to the whole group. A large group discussion facilitated by the consultant gained general agreement on the focus areas for the Push Agenda.

This final draft will be reviewed by other institutional stakeholder groups (e.g., student government, trustees, faculty senate) for final feedback and agreement before an implementation plan is created going forward.

A general timeline of one month was established for these review meetings to ensure some momentum was created and it didn't get lost in endless process.

This Push Agenda meeting accomplished several things:

1. It created a shared context for the group by using the Future Timeline.

2. Leaders then talked about what really needed to be moved forward over the next year. (Some objectives in the original plan did not move forward because they either didn't respond to changing events or there weren't sufficient resources to accomplish them.)

3. A constructive process for soliciting feedback about proposed ideas was created that further informed participants' thinking was created.

4. A small, diverse group of leaders worked the data carefully and created a second draft set of recommendations for the whole group. (This is a very effective practice that was suggested by the whole group to manage information overload and recognized that not everyone has to be involved in everything.) A final draft set of recommendations was presented, discussed, and approved by the whole leadership group.

5. The process was engaging, transparent, and built the confidence of participants because they believed that we were focusing on the right things in the final year of the plan.

We anonymously evaluated the retreat. It was overwhelmingly positive, and we shared the findings with all the participants. There were a couple of disgruntled participants who wanted to spend more time delving into the details, but overall, a success.

An Important Note:

As you can see throughout the book, I tend to emphasize *anonymously* evaluating the effectiveness of these practices and protocols. It is important for leaders to commit to doing this on a continual basis so that you get the most honest responses possible. There will be times when the results are not good—this is when you really have to share the feedback. It is respectful to participants and it builds credibility in the processes going forward.

You will almost always have some "cranky" people who are never satisfied. Strangely, we pay way more attention to these negative people than is ever warranted. In my experience, it's one of the great peculiarities of higher education. If you get anywhere near 80 percent of people that like these activities and find them helpful, you will "live with the gods" of implementation.

You always need to listen to everyone but be realistic about "satisfying" everyone because it's not possible.

A "COLLABORATIVE" STRATEGIC PLANNING PROCESS
A Five-Phase Model

The primary reason that I included this description of a collaborative planning process is that I have learned that it's *the process* that is key to successful implementation efforts. I have conducted several deep dives with campus clients (e.g., Saint Joseph's University, Anoka Ramsey Community College, Metropolitan State University, and Ohio Dominican University) to review the progress of their strategic plans. We have found that at the end of year three, 80 percent of the stated goals were accomplished.

Attention to the process of planning helps later with implementation because stakeholders actually "own" their plan and work hard to complete it.

This brief paper describes a five-phase "collaborative" strategic planning process that has worked in over 50 diverse institutions (e.g., Saint Joseph's University, Bellarmine University, The University of the West Indies, Eastern Illinois University, De Paul University, Frostburg University, University of California-Santa Cruz, Central Community College, The College of New Rochelle, Mount Saint Mary College, Anoka Ramsey Community College, The University of South Dakota) in higher education.

The process is highly engaging and inclusive in nature and efficient in its execution. The process is designed to create commitment to the implementation of the strategic plan from the very beginning. It is consultant "lite" and utilizes a highly credible internal planning task force as the driving mechanism for the entire process. It taps into and builds the capacity of the institution to think and plan in collaborative and inclusive ways. Campus stakeholders feel heard and valued as their meaningful involvement helps create a bright and robust future for the institution.

The five phases are:

1. Getting organized

2. Data gathering

3. Sense making

4. Vision conference(s)

5. Goals conference(s)

Guiding Principles/Essential Elements

1. Meaningful engagement of institutional stakeholders is at the heart of the process. By engagement we mean face-to-face inter-action and discussion.

2. Information gathered throughout the planning process is shared with everyone. Transparency is essential.

3. The role of the consultant(s) is to help tap into and build the capacity of the internal stakeholders and guide the planning process, not direct it.

4. Attention is paid to the *external* issues and trends in higher education throughout the process so that institutional stakeholders don't focus too much on their own world. (We call this listening to yourself too much.)

5. External stakeholders (alumni, community, business) are an important part of the process and are engaged in several phases of

the planning process. This creates a well-informed and robust plan that intelligently responds to the pace and complexity of change and responds to the different stakeholder interests that surrounds every institution.

Establishing the Planning Task Force (PTF)

The key to the success of a collaborative strategic planning process is a highly credible task force. The composition of the PTF will make or break the planning effort. Each task force member must have an excellent reputation and be willing to work hard over the course of the planning process. The PTF is both a thinking *and* doing group.

It is best to have two cochairs, preferably a highly credible faculty member and a high level administrator (e.g., CBO, Vice President). Selecting the cochairs is the first strategic thing the president does and will communicate volumes about the importance of the planning process and its potential for success. Choose wisely. The external consultant talks with the PTF cochairs biweekly to ensure quality communication.

The ideal number of task force members is somewhere between 40 and 50 highly credible individuals. Although we have worked with task forces of 60 plus, it can be challenging to work with such a large group.

Getting Organized

It takes effective planning and organization to operationalize a collaborative strategic planning process. Good beginnings are essential to the success of the process; therefore, the president must do several things to ensure that an effective and efficient planning process takes place:

1. Communicate to the campus that the strategic planning process is important to the future of the institution and show their real interest, if not, enthusiasm for an inclusive, participative, and transparent process. This has to be done throughout the process and not just at the beginning.

2. Establish a highly credible strategic planning task force (PTF).

3. Commit the technological resources to the planning process to ensure that everyone knows how to be involved, can contribute their ideas and feedback to the process, and be fully informed through planning updates.

4. Clarify his or her role in the planning process as a champion and supporter but not a driver or controller of the process.

5. Visibly and authentically support the process by attending training sessions, communicating with the diverse stakeholder groups throughout the campus about the process, and most importantly, listening to people's concerns and aspirations.

6. The composition must reflect the diversity of the institution.

7. Try and avoid the "usual suspects" and include some individuals who rarely are asked to the table.

8. Include "informal leaders" who may not have a title but have huge peer influence.

9. Each member should have an excellent reputation and respect for the institution.

10. The "mix" should be about 60 percent faculty and 40 percent staff and administrators. It is essential that faculty believe that they are well represented or your planning process will probably fail.

Try to include one or two "curmudgeons"—those individuals who are known for their skeptical attitudes and are most willing to share them. They also tend to be credible members of the community and care about the place and the mission. This will help provide rigor and credibility to the process. Do not have deeply cynical individuals on the task force. They will never be convinced of its authenticity and will only drag the process down. Skeptics are welcome—cynics need not apply.

The President's Cabinet should be well represented on the task force because, at the end of the day, they will be charged to implement it.

This is an essential element to remember. The cabinet will "inherit" the strategic plan once all the hard work and thinking has been completed. The last thing you want is a cabinet that doesn't feel ownership for the implementation of the plan because they were not meaningfully involved in creating it.

Initial responsibilities of the task force include:

1. Establishing a calendar of events for the year.

2. Developing a communication plan.

3. Identifying forums for engagement and data gathering (e.g., faculty senate meetings, staff and administrative councils, student government, community groups, alumni gatherings, etc.).

4. Learning about collaborative planning and meeting designs that engage stakeholders thinking and passions.

Data Gathering and Engagement

The heart of collaborative planning is the meaningful engagement of stakeholders throughout the institution. Engagement means face-to-face interaction, discussion, and dialogue. Although surveys have a role in any planning process, they are secondary in this kind of planning.

At the beginning of the planning process, a consultant works with the entire planning task force for two full days and shares a wide variety of highly interactive planning activities. Each of the activities creates real data from PTF members *and* teaches them how to utilize the activities. It is expected that once the PTF members experience the effectiveness and efficacy of the planning activities, they will then go out and engage a variety of stakeholders throughout the institution. A Stakeholder Review is conducted to provide a clear picture of who needs to be connected to and informed about the planning process as it moves forward.

Before the end of the second day, task force members organize themselves and create an engagement plan for the next two months. They will work in pairs to support each other and will engage faculty, staff, and administrators throughout the campus as well as external stake-holders. It is rather easy to meaningfully engage well over a thousand people over the course of two months.

Building the capacity of the task force members to implement the collaborative planning process does several things: 1) the task force members "own" the process because they are at the heart of it; 2) internal stakeholders witness their own people working hard to create an effective planning process; 3) it builds tremendous credibility for the planning process because it is something that is led by insiders and not by outsiders; 4) it builds the ongoing capacity of the task force members to continue to do collaborative planning in their own departments (e.g., self-studies) and administrative units after the planning process is completed; and 5) it saves a lot of money because insiders, not consultants, do most of the work.

Sense Making

After the PTF has conducted dozens of interactive meetings through-out and beyond the campus, there will be a great deal of information generated. All the data that is gathered goes into a centralized data-base for planning task force members to review. At this stage, the PTF spends a full day reporting out their findings and agree on the strategic themes for the planning process (e.g., Academic Excellence, Diversity and Inclusion, The Role of Collaborative Research, Innovation and Creativity, Community & Culture). Selecting the themes for planning is a transparent process that involves the entire PTF. Usually, five to six themes are selected to help focus the planning process.

Implementation Note:

In my experience, if you have more than five to six big, strategic themes, your implementation efforts will be challenged, even if you have the financial resources needed. People can only pay attention to a handful of big ideas and move them forward effectively. If you look at the top 20 or 30 campuses across the country who have many re-sources, you will find that most have five to six big Strategic Themes or Goals.

After the strategic themes have been agreed upon, *Concept Papers* are then written to describe the strategic themes and their importance to the institution. The writing of the concept papers does several things: 1) they put some boundaries around the most important issues that need to be in the institution's strategic plan (everything cannot be in the plan); 2) it distills the information gathered during the planning process into "chewable chunks" so that stakeholders can be informed about the issues and not deluged with too much information; and 3) they are used to educate attendees at the future Vision Conference.

Concept papers are approximately five pages in length and layperson friendly. Their purpose is to educate people about a particular issue, not dazzle them with big words or complicated explanations. The papers provide a historical context about the issue and identifies regional, national, and if appropriate, international perspectives about the issues and clearly describes how campus stakeholders see the issue from all the data gathering that has taken place.

The concept papers are generally written by PTF members but they can utilize outsiders to help write them. All concept papers are reviewed by task force members and then sent out to the community at large via the campus intranet. During the writing of the concept papers there is a great deal of discussion and dialogue between PTF members. When the concept papers are finally produced, there is clear ownership of the information.

The Vision Conference

The Vision Conference is a highly interactive, one-day meeting involving somewhere between 50–75 stakeholders. Attendees at the conference are 70 percent internal (all the planning task force members attend) and 30 percent external stakeholders. The main reason you invite external stakeholders (e.g., alumni, business community, neighborhood leaders) is to ensure that the institution has an external perspective in the room as they think about the future. In planning circles we have a saying, "You want to avoid listening to yourselves too much." The external stakeholders will provide a different (not better) perspective that can help the campus think more broadly.

In a large institution, you would have several one-day vision conferences rather than a large one with 100 plus participants. If you have too many people, it can feel like herding cats and there will be less interaction within the group because of the large numbers.

There are three distinct elements to a Vision Conference:

1. **Review of the Concept Papers and Discussion**

   A highly engaging meeting design is utilized so that all conference participants have a chance to review the concept papers and glean the essential themes from each one. This usually takes two hours and helps ensure that all participants are well informed about the institutional issues *before* they think about the future of the institution. A Vision Conference is not a blue sky, brainstorming session. It is grounded in quality information and institutional realities. The Concept Paper Review creates a shared experience and database for participants and helps set the stage for creating a "preferred" future.

2. **A Stakeholder Review**

   The main reason you invite a diverse set of stakeholders to the Vision Conference is to be informed by their unique and distinct perspectives. The more institutional leaders understand how different people see the institution, the more informed they are. You want to paint a robust future picture of the institution and that can only happen if a wide range of perspectives are shared and understood.

   A Stakeholder Review involves the different stakeholders at the Vision Conference (faculty, students, business, community, etc.) organizing themselves and having a discussion about how they see the institution's future. The output of their discussion is four to five important ideas and themes from their *unique* stakeholder perspective that they would like to share with the other participants at the conference. Sharing the very different perspectives expands participants' thinking, creates the opportunity to understand what is important to others, and develops a more robust thinking pool of ideas.

Note 1: At one Vision Conference, the business community communicated that were happy with the intellectual skills of the graduating students at the university but that they needed more students who could work effectively on teams and build relationships with others. The information greatly influenced the future pictures of the institution because participants realized that they needed to redesign their curriculum to actually teach about teams, collaboration, and cross-boundary work.

Note 2: At another conference, the business community communicated that they wanted a more assertive presence of the university in their organizations. We don't just need graduates, we need research, new business models, strategies, consulting, etc. For example, in a Vision Conference, for Research 1 institution, the local business community stated that they needed help with new ways to deal with their perennial water shortage and requested that some partnerships be created to create news strategies to deal with this complex issue.

Note 3: At a recent Vision Conference, the parents group communicated to everyone at the conference that they were very pleased how their children were doing at the school and reminded participants that students need intellectual challenge, and support and nurturing. Please educate the "whole student " was their request.

3. **Creating a "Preferred Future"**

The culminating exercise of the Conference is creating shared pictures of the future. We have found that utilizing a five-year framework seems to work best because it allows participants to do some horizon thinking while still grounded in current reality. Participants work in small diverse groups of six to eight people (faculty, business, students, staff, etc.) and create shared pictures of the future based on the strategic themes from the concept papers. If *Diversity and Inclusion* were a strategic theme, we would ask them to describe what Diversity and Inclusion really looks like on our campus five years from now. If *Collaborative Research* were a strategic theme, we would ask them to identify the new research areas we have explored over the past five years.

After the Preferred Futures are created, each group makes a presentation to the whole group. (With large conferences of 75–100 people, a design is created so that the small groups work with another group to share their future pictures and agree on a shared picture together. This way you avoid 10 plus presentations.) After the presentations, a facilitated discussion helps identify the many common ground ideas and themes from all the shared pictures. These elements are used to create a draft Vision Statement for the institution that goes out to the campus for review and refinement.

The planning task force usually charges a small group to write a draft vision statement and take responsibility for incorporating the feedback that is received into a final vision statement.

The Goals Conference

Approximately one month after the Vision Conference, the planning task force convenes for one day to create a broad implementation plan for the institution. At this time, other stakeholders outside of the PTF are invited to lend their expertise and energy to creating the goals. Often, these are individuals who will be charged with implementing the strategic plan.

Participants utilize the new vision statement to create a set of strategic goals for each of the strategic themes (e.g., Diversity and Inclusion, Academic Excellence, Collaborative Research). After the goals have been agreed upon, Action Plans are created for each strategic goal. Feedback processes are built into the conference to make sure that all participants share their advice and ideas in creating the Action Plans.

If there is not enough time to complete the Action Plans, a process for completion is established before participants leave the conference. The draft Action Plan usually goes to the President's Cabinet for discussion and review. It usually takes another month or so to produce a detailed Implementation Plan.

Summary

General Timeline: One Year

1. Organizing the Process = two months

2. Data Gathering and Engagement = three months

3. Sense Making = two to three months

4. Vision Conference = one to two months

5. Goals Conference = one to two months[51]

I hope that the reader finds this book useful and practical. I have tried to share things that have actually worked on multiple campuses. Lifting things up and moving them forward is hard and noble work. We need to get much better at recognizing and rewarding the "doers"—they are the true heroes in my opinion. We have way too many "visionaries" who actually don't do much.

If you have any questions about the ideas in this book, please feel free to contact me at sanaghan@aol.com. If you have a challenge and want to walk through it with a thought partner, I would be honored to help (**no charge**!). If you have used something in this book that you found helpful, please share that with me also. Lastly, if you had a problem with some of these practices and protocols, I want to hear about them also. The learning journey continues. Good Luck!

Pat Sanaghan, 2021

---

51 Sanaghan, P. *Collaborative Strategic Planning.*

Annotated Bibliography

The following articles, monographs, and books are resources for interested readers to consider as they endeavor to learn how to implement their strategic plan. This is not meant to be a comprehensive list, just some readings I have found very helpful in my own learning journey.

 Note: Almost all of these are from the "corporate" sector but their translation to higher education is easy to make. The "business" world has to execute and implement well or they don't survive. I strongly believe we can learn some things from their thinking and approaches. I believe that they will.

1. Royer, Isabelle, "Why Bad Projects Are So Hard to Kill," *Harvard Business Review* 81, no. 2 (2003): 48-56.

    Excellent article highlighting one of the embedded challenges facing effective implementation efforts. The author explains that often managers and leaders charge ahead with a project or initiative in face of mounting evidence that success is pretty well unachievable. There is a fervent and widespread belief among managers of the inevitability of their project's ultimate success.

    Although optimism can be helpful, faith can blind you from increasingly negative feedback. Curiously, the author found in her research that setbacks, rather than undermining faith, often drive people to work all the harder to maintain it. Many leaders become "true believers" with an unyielding conviction that their project will be successful, despite the odds. Often, if the leader is charismatic, credible, or likable, their strong belief becomes a collective belief that takes on a life of its own.

Her solution is to identify "exit champions" who have the temperament and credibility to question whether a project is working or not by using real data, not aspirations, to decide if a project or initiative should be shut down.

In higher education, we are great at adding but not so good at subtracting or stopping something from moving forward. Although "exit champions" are rare in higher education, it is an idea worth considering, especially at the cabinet level. In the example of the Student First program in the book, having an "exit" champion during the first of three attempts would have been a good idea.

Note: The "Opportunity Map" design in the Systems chapter can be a useful tool to utilize when assessing projects going forward. You might use some different criteria to assess each project or initiative. For example, if a project is slowing down or in trouble, some questions you might ask are:

a.   What's the level of confidence you have with this project going forward?

b.   Do we have enough resources to complete this project?

c.   Do we have enough talent to move this project forward?

2.   Matta, Nadim E., and Ronald N. Ashkenas. "Why Good Projects Fail Anyway," *Harvard Business Review* 81, no. 9 (2003): 109-114.

The authors tell us that big projects fail at an astonishing rate— well over half of them. They identify three "risks" to successful implementation:

a.   **Whitespace:** This happens when planners leave gaps in the project plan by failing to anticipate all the project's required activities and work streams.

b. **Execution:** Project teams fail to carry out designated activities properly.

c. **Integration:** This is where team members execute all tasks flawlessly, on time, and within budget but don't know all the projects that are working in tandem and are unable then to bring it all together. The result is that the project doesn't deliver the intended results.

They suggest a "rapid results" approach where small projects are initiated to quickly deliver mini-versions of the big project's end results. These become learning projects where the project teams can iron out kinks early on and on a small scale. The key is that these *rapid results* initiatives produce measurable results on a small scale. They are not theoretical scenarios but on-the-ground projects that teams can implement and learn from.

These "rapid" or fast initiatives have a few key elements:

They run less than 100 days.

There is a real sense of urgency attached to them. They are designed to deliver quick wins.

Most importantly, they stimulate creativity.

These rapid initiatives enable people to discover what's working and what isn't and learn as they go. They can also produce real results. This article is stimulating and counterintuitive.

I believe that higher education leaders should consider some of these ideas because we need to be more agile and nimble going forward and can't wait for the "perfect" solution. This is a reality that the COVID-19 pandemic will determine for us going forward. We will have to be smart *and* faster, if we are going to thrive in the future.

3. Bungay, Stephen. *The Art of Action: How Leaders Close the Gaps Between Plans, Actions, and Results* (London: Nicholas Brealey Publishing, 2011).

This is an excellent book; in fact, it is one of the very best I have read in the implementation field and helps resolve one of the greatest implementation challenges: *lots of activity going on but no real outcomes.*

The author communicates the essential question that people in organizations ask their leaders: "What do you want me to do?" This might sound simple but it strikes at the heart of execution. If people don't understand what is expected of them, successful implementation is impossible. In addition, people have to understand the rationale or the "why" of what they are being asked to implement. This sounds simple but often leaders are poor at providing the meaningful "why."

Bungay also shares that people need to understand their decision level authority—what they can or can't do. He provides powerful and practical advice on implementation and understands how difficult it is to actually accomplish something meaningful in our organizations.

4. Neilson, Gary L., Karla L. Martin, and Elizabeth Powers. "The Secrets to Successful Strategy Execution," *Harvard Business Review* 86 (2008): 60–70.

The authors conducted extensive research with 31 different companies and have identified 17 fundamental traits of organizational effectiveness. This creates a comprehensive framework for leaders who are interested in becoming what they call a "resilient" organization.

Although they share 17 different traits, four of them are essential to organizational effectiveness:

a. Clarifying the *decision rights* in order for people to understand what they can and cannot do. Clarifying the level of authority facilitates quicker implementation. (Remember the five levels of Decision-Making in Chapter 4.)

b. Creating powerful *information flows* so people can get the information they need when they need it.

c. Having a "scorecard," or a way to measure progress toward stated goals, is a critical element along with the appropriate incentives, rewards, and recognition.

d. Organizing the *structures* to facilitate effective implementation is the last of the final four traits. Usually leaders start to "reorganize" and redesign their organizations to improve execution efforts first. The authors strongly suggest that should not be done until decision rights are clear, information is available and the metrics in place. Then start to organize the company to facilitate execution.

5. Bakke, Dennis, *The Decision Maker: Unlock the Potential of Everyone in Your Organization, One Decision at a Time* (Seattle: Pear Press, 2013).

This is an excellent resource for leaders who are interested in pushing decision-making down to where it belongs. The author tells us that people are making decisions all the time and that we need to trust them to make good decisions. He prefers the leader as "coach" who provides support advice and asks good questions but lets the players play.

He provides an "advice process" where people seek out the ideas, expertise, and perspectives of others *before* they make important decisions. The bigger the decision, the more people you ask. Sounds simple but it is an excellent approach to decision-making and implementation. When decision-making is pushed upstairs, far from the field of play, implementation efforts tend to falter.

This is not a "soft" or touchy-feely approach to decision-making; it has rigor and clarity and, most importantly, it works. The author has been the CEO of two large and complex organizations where he actually used this approach successfully. It provides a powerful, different, and collaborative approach to effective decision-making, which enables implementation to occur.

6. Gast, Arne, and Michele Zanini, "The Social Side of Strategy," *McKinsey Quarterly* 82 (2012): 82–93.

This is an excellent white paper from McKinsey, which offers solid, informative research on implementation. The authors firmly believe that "radical inclusion" is needed when establishing and vetting strategic plans. Strategy that is handed down from the top has a miserable track record and they believe by meaningfully involving others you increase the probability that you will actually accomplish something. People need to "embrace" the strategy before they can implement it. Other researchers and practitioners (Sanaghan, 2009, Hbreniak, 2013, McKnight, Kaney, & Breur, 2013, Sanaghan & Mrig, 2015) are aligned with this thinking.

They suggest leaders provide the social technology tools to include people throughout the organization, especially leaders on the "fringe" (those who think differently but have credibility with their peers).

They also believe that leaders need to organize cross-boundary discussions with people throughout their organization and provide a "radical transparency" of information across the company. They provide several excellent examples of organizations that meaningfully involved, not hundreds but thousands, of stakeholders in creating, shaping, and crafting their organization's strategy.

This *radical inclusion* creates a great deal of ideas but, most importantly, produces *insight* regarding the competition, the larger organization, and ways to collaborate across boundaries. The authors highlight one of the essential but not widely discussed challenges facing implementation, the social side. Things get done through the hard work of people, and the more they understand what's going on in the organization and are able to share their ideas and passions, the more real work will get done. Relational capital is essential to successful implementation.

7. Covey, Stephen R., Bob Whitman, and Breck England, *Predictable Results in Unpredictable Times* (Salt Lake City: FranklinCovey Publishing, 2009).

This is an excellent book full of informative models, frameworks, and advice that leaders interested in implementation will find practical and useful. The authors have identified several critical elements of winning companies who know how to execute:

    a. **They have simple, clear goals:** people understand what their organization is trying to accomplish.

    b. They **repeatedly revisit their goals:** They realize the environment is constantly changing and can influence their organization in many ways. They monitor progress towards goals and make sure everyone is on the same page.

    c. They have **clear targets** that are reachable and doable. People understand the specific things they need to accomplish and have faith they can actually accomplish them.

    d. They have **strong follow through** and constantly monitor progress, provide supportive supervision, and hold their people accountable.

    e. They **measure results**. Each unit understands their "scorecard" and feedback towards progress is provided.

    f. The biggest gift the authors provide is their deep insight into the importance of **trust** in organizational life and, especially, implementation efforts.

They use the metaphors of *trust, taxes*, and *trust dividends* and believe trust always affects two measurable outcomes: S**peed** and **cost**. When trust in an organization is high, things move quickly. When trust is low, things move at a snail's pace and everything gets more expensive.

These metaphors apply to higher education as well. In most of my work on campuses, I have found the trust level pretty high, which aids implementation efforts. I have worked with several where trust was low and relationships were contentious. They are difficult places to be and progress is slow and often painful.

If leaders can learn effective ways to build and nurture trust in their organizations, they will achieve powerful results.

8. Edmondson, Amy C., "Strategies For Learning From Failure," *Harvard Business Review* 89, no. 4 (2011): 48–55.

The author believes we are programmed from an early age to think failure is bad and this false belief prevents organizations from learning effectively from their missteps. With implementation efforts, failure is inevitable so using these opportunities as sources of strategic information is just a smart thing to do.

The author highlights nine reasons for failure, ranging from lack of ability, to not being able to deal with uncertainty, to actual deviance where a person chooses to violate a prescribed process or practice. These nine reasons enable leaders to "unpack" the reasons for failure and identify specific strategies to learn from.

Although learning from failures requires different strategies in different work settings, the ultimate goal should be to detect them early, analyze them well, and learn from them so you can apply the new experience to current and future efforts.

But for the organization to be successful and use failure as a resource, employees must feel safe admitting to them and reporting them. She believes creating that kind of environment takes strong leadership. Other leaders, researchers, and theorists like Bossidy & Charan, 2002, Hrebiniak, 2005, 2013, Covey, 2008, and Fukiyama, 1995, concur with this finding.

9. Bryan, Lowell L., Eric Matson, and Leigh M. Weiss. "Harnessing the Power of Informal Employee Networks," *McKinsey Quarterly* no. 4 (2007): 44–55.

If we are going to accomplish important things on our campuses, cross-boundary collaboration will be essential to our overall success. We will need to be world class at sharing best practices, identifying systemic issues, and solving them, making sure people know who to go to for advice, experience, resources, and help.

The authors note that *informal* networks are powerful sources of collaboration *across* thick silo walls, but as ad hoc structures, their performance depends on serendipity and *they can't be managed.* They recognize that many large, complex organizations have dozens, if not hundreds, of informal networks where people share ideas and collaborate. The challenge is what do you do with these various networks so that the organization becomes smarter and actually accomplishes meaningful things?

The authors propose *formalizing* the networks by giving them a *leader*, focusing their interactions on *specific topics,* and building an *infrastructure* that stimulates the ongoing exchange of ideas (e.g., councils, communities of practice, peer groups).

Informal networks often have crucial members who serve as hubs to connect participants, which is also described in the article, "The Social Side of Strategy," but such members can hobble, even undermine, the network if they become overloaded, act as gatekeepers, horde knowledge to gain power, or leave the company. In short, they can't be managed well and formal structures and protocols need to be established in order to facilitate the work of the informal groups.

The specific objective of designing and establishing formal networks is to increase the value and lower the costs of collaboration throughout the organization. Formal networks create pathways for the natural exchange of information and knowledge. Individual members don't have to find one another through serendipity—they know who to contact and where to find others.

To formalize a network, the company must define who will lead it. The leader needs to act as a "servant leader" to help members improve their performance. Assessment processes need to

be established to determine the satisfaction of members and the effectiveness of the network.

I believe this is an important idea that should be developed on many of our campuses. These networks can be powerful assets but need care and attention or they will become "stranded" assets. The article provides some meaningful strategies that higher education leaders need to consider.

Note: Note the "Adhocracy Design" in the Systems 2 chapter to help identify a powerful network of "doers."

10. McChesney, Chris, Sean Covey, and Jim Huling, *The 4 Disciplines of Execution: Achieving Your Wildly Important Goals* (New York: Free Press, 2012).

The authors use a powerful metaphor they call "the whirlwind" to describe the massive amount of energy it takes to keep an organization functioning and things moving. They believe about 80 percent of our time, energy, and attention is consumed by the daily grind or "the whirlwind." That leaves us with only 20 percent of our time to get important and strategic work accomplished.

This metaphor resonates deeply with me and describes my experience with campuses well. Given that we only have this 20 percent, we need to be disciplined and focused if we are going to be able to actually implement things.

They provide four disciplines to help leaders with getting important things accomplished:

a. **Focusing on the wildly important:** Execution starts with focus—without it, the other three disciplines won't help you. The *wildly important goal* (the WIG) is a goal that can make all the difference and you have to commit to applying a disproportionate amount of energy to it. They believe leaders must identify the one area where change would have the greatest impact and provide some guidelines on how to identify this priority area.

b. **Act on lead measures:** While a *lag* measure tells you if you have achieved your goal (e.g., graduation rates, number of students getting a job after graduation), a *lead* measure tells you if you are *likely* to achieve the goal. A lead measure is *predictive*—if you influence these, then your lag measures will also be impacted. For example, if your freshman retention rate plummets or increases, it will impact your graduation rate. It is a very different way of thinking because it asks you to identify all the specific measures, tasks, and activities needed to accomplish a goal. Once you do this, you can apply resources, thinking and attention on influencing the lead measures and not waiting for the lag measures to see if you were successful.

   c. **Keep a compelling scorecard:** This third discipline makes sure that everyone knows the scores at all times so that they can tell if they are winning or not. People disengage when they don't know the "score" and a powerful, visual scorecard can be an effective enabler and motivator. They advise to: 1) keep the scorecard simple, 2) make sure it can be seen easily and is understandable, and 3) make sure it shows lead and lag measures.

   d. **Create a cadence of accountability:** The authors believe leaders must establish a recurring cycle of accountability for past performance and ways to move the score forward on a continuous basis. This discipline is where execution happens. The first three disciplines set up the game but until you apply this discipline, you are not in the game. Once again, they provide specific strategies to create a "cadence of accountability."

This is an outstanding book, full of practical and doable strategies and advice for leaders who want to create an implementation culture.

11. Cross, Ross, and Laurence Prusak. "The People Who Make Organizations Go or Stop, *Harvard Business Review* 80, no. 6 (2002): 104–111.

Leaders who are excellent with execution and implementation will find this article more reinforcing than enlightening. Any leader who is successful at accomplishing the important things in their organization understands how important individuals and personal networks are to the implementation process.

The authors believe the real work in most companies is done informally through personal contacts and that it is possible to develop these informal networks systemically in service of large organizational goals. (The McKinsey paper, "Harnessing the Power of Informal Employee Networks" supports this notion.)

They identify four common role players whose performance is critical to the productivity of any organization:

a. Central connectors

b. Boundary spanners

c. Information brokers

d. Peripheral specialists

These role players are important *and* almost invisible to senior leaders. This is an essential thing for senior leaders to understand. Often, the people who can help you the most are concealed from your view. The most important step in managing these informal networks is to bring them into the open through a process called, "social network analysis," which identifies these key people and begins to organize them.

The authors provide specific advice and strategies to tap these networks and build organizational capacity. These four different role players are similar to the adhocracy I mentioned in the book. Identify and utilize these individuals and networks so that you can implement your strategic plan.

12. Connors, Roger, and Tom Smith, *How Did That Happen?: Holding People Accountable for Results the Positive, Principled Way* (New York: Portfolio/Penguin, 2011).

The authors provide some interesting thinking about holding people accountable in a positive and principled way. They use the metaphor of an "accountability sequence" to describe their interesting

approach. They talk about an "outer ring" where you form, communicate, align, and inspect expectations. This important conversation attempts to get all the players on the same page with clear and shared expectations for performance. They also describe the "inner ring" where you engage in an "accountability conversation" to determine the best way to deal with unmet expectations.

The authors also describe the top five reasons why people don't hold each other accountable and it is enlightening:

- **Reason 1:** We have a fear of offending someone *or* jeopardizing a personal relationship.

- **Reason 2:** We often have a feeling that we lack the time to follow up effectively. Why raise the issue if you can't pay attention to it over time?

- **Reason 3:** We often lack the faith that the effort expended to hold others accountable will make enough of a difference.

- **Reason 4:** We worry that by holding someone accountable we might expose our own shortcomings.

- **Reason 5:** We often have a reluctance to speak out and suffer retaliation. (Most of us have seen someone attempt to hold others "accountable," suffer personal attacks ("Who does he think he is, Mr. Perfect?") or political fallout because the person who was held accountable is "connected" to power.)

Note: I think that the reasons stated above are highly relevant to the higher education context. When you add in the powerful collegiality in higher education, I think it adds additional challenges for holding people accountable.

The authors share some effective advice on detecting when an "accountability conversation" isn't going well and offers some strategies on how to deal with a conversation that is going south or a person who is good at dodging responsibility.

They provide a helpful checklist they call the "Form" checklist to help supervisors build an accountability framework with their employees:

a. **Is it frameable?** To ensure the expectation is consistent with the current vision, strategy, and business priorities.

b. **Is it obtainable?** Need to ensure the expectation is achievable in terms of current resources and capacity constraints. This is an important reality check because people will either buy in or buy out if they believe their assignments are/are not achievable.

c. **Is it respectable?** Are the expectations "portable?" Can they clearly be communicated throughout the organization?

d. **Is it measurable?** Need to ensure that progress toward achieving expectations can be tracked and the fulfillment of expectations can be measured.

13. Bossidy, Larry, Ram Charan, and Charles Burck, *Execution: The Discipline of Getting Things Done* (London: Random House Business, 2011).

I believe this is one of the very best books on implementation and execution ever written. The authors believe execution is "the" great-unaddressed issue in the business world today. But don't let this mislead you; execution lives large in higher education also.

The authors (one of them was the CEO of Honeywell and the other a world class organizational consultant) believe too many leaders place too much emphasis on what some call high level strategy and philosophy and not enough time on implementation. (Hrebiniak, 2013 is also aligned with this thinking.)

They state:

a. That execution is a discipline and integral to strategy.

b. It is the major job of the business leadership.

c.   It must be a core element of an organization's culture.

For them, execution is a systematic process for rigorously discussing the hows and whys, questioning, tenaciously following through, and ensuring accountability. Even though the authors sound disciplined with their notions, they are well aware of the people side of execution and promote a humane process that is supportive, honest, and decent to people.

The heart of execution lies in three proposed processes:

a.   The people process.

b.   The strategy process.

c.   The operations process.

The authors detail each process in layperson friendly terms that help create a coherent whole for leaders. All three processes must be paid attention to diligently and repeatedly.

They highlight seven essential leadership behaviors that help facilitate execution:

a.   Know your people and your business.

b.   Insist on realism.

c.   Set clear goals and priorities.

d.   Follow through on commitments.

e.   Reward the doers.

f.   Expand people's capabilities, develop and teach them.

g.   Know yourself.

They provide advice on organizational protocols and mechanisms needed to ensure accountability, dialogue, and implementation. They are able to share ways to influence the individual, the team, work unit, and organization toward developing a culture of execution.

I believe this book is an important *leadership* book, and should be on the desk, not bookshelf, of every leader on campus. It is an outstanding resource and a great "book club" conversation starter.

Made in the USA
Middletown, DE
26 September 2023